JUST GO

Ginger,

Happy Travels!

JUST GO

A Globetrotting Guide to
Travel Like an Expert, Connect
Like a Local, and Live the
Adventure of a Lifetime

DREW BINSKY

BenBella Books, Inc.
Dallas, TX

BenBella Books, Inc.
10440 N. Central Expressway
Suite 800
Dallas, TX 75231
benbellabooks.com
Send feedback to feedback@benbellabooks.com

BenBella is a federally registered trademark.

Printed in the United States of America
10 9 8 7 6 5 4 3 2 1

Library of Congress Control Number: 2023044567
ISBN 9781637742693 (trade paperback)
ISBN 9781637742709 (ebook)

Editing by Kristen McGuinness and Claire Schulz
Copyediting by Scott Calamar
Proofreading by Jenny Bridges and Ashley Casteel
Indexing by WordCo Indexing Services
Text design and composition by PerfecType
Cover design by Sarah Avinger
Cover image © Adobe Stock / lubashka (globe)
Logo and top cover photo courtesy of the author
Cover photos by Deanna Goldberg (top) and Unsplash / Alexander Schimmeck (bottom)
Printed by Lake Book Manufacturing

Special discounts for bulk sales are available. Please contact bulkorders@benbellabooks.com.

For my parents

CONTENTS

📍 Antelope Canyon, USA

📍 Panam Nagar, Bangladesh   📍 Cairo, Egypt

START HERE

The day is July 25, 2020. I was supposed to step foot in my 197th country two months ago, completing my quest to travel to every country in the world, but since March 2020 I've been stuck at home with six countries left, and I have no idea when I'm going to cross the finish line. I can't believe that after visiting over 95 percent of the world's countries, that world had shut down. Like everyone, I am anxious and concerned about the pandemic, but also, I have been trapped. I only have six more countries to complete my goal—Venezuela, Ecuador, Jamaica, Saudi Arabia, Ghana, and Palau—and though we are just beginning to get on planes again, I am determined to finish what I started.

So today, on this hot and eerily quiet July day, I am finally back in an airport. The international terminal at LAX is *dead*. I've never really imagined an airport with nobody inside of it before, and yet that's almost what I'm experiencing. It feels like I've entered a postapocalyptic scene—every single restaurant and store is closed, the walls are bedecked with hand sanitizer containers, below my feet are little circular signs telling me to keep a six-foot distance, and most of the chairs are covered with plastic wrap. I'm not sure what to think, but I do know that there are stories out there to be told, and right now, no one else is telling them. But will it be worth it?

What do you think?

Do I travel in the middle of a global pandemic?

Do I go back home and not finish my mission?

Do I document the world so that others can see what happened?

Do I get on the plane?

Spoiler: I always get on the plane.

Nineteen months and forty-seven plane rides later, the world looked different, and I finally crossed those final six countries off my list, joining a small but passionate club of around 250 globe-trotting travelers who have successfully completed their mission to visit all 197 countries in the world. Whether you share the same goal or you're just planning to travel a bit off the beaten path, I'm looking forward to going along with you on your journey—helping you to become a better traveler and save money in the process.

Welcome to *Just Go*, where I'll be sharing secrets from visiting every country in the world so you can visit *any* country in the world.

> **Because what I've learned from always getting on the plane is that the world is a lot more connected, accessible, and safer than you think.**

You see, traveling wasn't something I got to do when I was a kid. We weren't that kind of family. But ever since my tenth birthday, when I was given a touch-lamp globe, I craved the adventure that I knew, for sure, was happening out there in the world. Every night before I went to bed, I would spin it and memorize every country and capital, dreaming of visiting faraway corners of the planet. I instantly became hooked on geography and learning about places outside my own borders, but I never had the chance to travel beyond North America until I was twenty years old and in college.

My junior year, I finally had a choice. I could stay at the University of Wisconsin, or I could study abroad. That fall, I headed to Prague in the Czech Republic for the most life-changing six months of my life. The moment my plane touched down at Prague's airport on a cold winter day in January 2012, I knew that I would be traveling for the long haul. I didn't know anyone in my study abroad program, nor was I really aware of anything happening in the Czech Republic. I just went there because I knew that with a three- to five-hour bus or train ride, I could also see the rest of Europe. I wanted to see *everything*. And I gave it my best shot. I was instantly hooked. I became obsessed with every part of the study abroad experience, from meeting new friends, to trying new foods, to partying at nightclubs and experiencing the European lifestyle. Our program included about fifty students, all randomly chosen from various universities across the US. Over the course of the semester, I visited fourteen countries in Europe and then six more on a one-month backpacking trip when our classes ended. I felt a sense of belonging in places I had never been. And though there were times when I got lost or I didn't know where I was going to stay the night, I felt safe.

Now, I'm going to get this out of the way on page one (or whatever page we happen to be on). I am well aware I am a white, American male—Jewish, but white and male nonetheless—who is traveling across the world.

I hold a US passport, which is the eighth-strongest passport in the world, allowing me to visit 186 countries and territories without needing to apply for a visa. For comparison, my wife, Deanna, holds a Philippines passport and can only visit sixty-three countries and territories without needing a visa. But obviously, my advantages extend beyond my documentation. Ever since my first days of travel, I recognized how being all of those things—white, American, and male—made it easier for me to travel, but also, I've known other white, American males who didn't necessarily know how to do it. Because what I have also seen, even in those first days of my traveling experiences, is that no matter your gender, language, race, or ethnicity, being curious about another culture always opens doors that might have otherwise been closed.

HOW I BECAME A TRAVEL BLOGGER
(PS—YOU CAN TOO)

At the tail end of my studies in Prague, I found a really cheap flight to Dubai and booked it spontaneously, not realizing what was in store for me. I arrived there dazed and confused. I was seeing all of the signs in Arabic, which to my uninitiated eyes looked like little squiggly lines; many women were covered in black attire from head to toe. One night, as I was sitting in front of the Burj Khalifa—the world's tallest building—I had an epiphany. It was May 20, 2012, and I was watching the fountain show outside the Burj, which puts the Bellagio in Las Vegas to shame. I knew I wanted to start my own business, but now I knew what I wanted to build that business around—I had discovered my life's passion, even though I was only in college, and clearly it has stuck. That passion was travel.

I had an idea to start a travel app that connected travelers (like myself) with locals in various cities around the world, so both parties could benefit from making new friends and having a cultural exchange. For the entire flight home over the Atlantic, I was frantically writing a business plan in my small notebook. I would call the app "Abroadify."

However, my plan soon shifted (and it wouldn't be the last unexpected turn on that journey).

My best friend, Sophie, who I met in Prague, told me about an opportunity to teach English in South Korea. I knew I didn't want to become a teacher—but I had never been to Asia before, and I saw it as a gateway to get myself out there—and to get to know the region and its people in a way being a tourist would have never offered me.

A month after graduating college with a double major in economics and entrepreneurship, I was on a plane to Seoul. I arrived there alone, once again, but it wasn't like landing in Prague or Dubai—the culture shock was huge. My co-teacher, Mrs. Kim, picked me up at the airport on a Friday afternoon, driving me one hour south of Seoul to a village called Jinsa-Ri, where I would now be living. She dropped me off at my new studio apartment and said: "See you on Monday for your first day of class."

I will never forget that feeling of being totally alone, lost in translation, purposeless for two days and without a working phone or an internet connection. The first thing I did was walk to the local supermarket, but I had no idea what was happening around me. I basically looked at all the photos on the food boxes to choose what my meals would be for the weekend: plain noodles, kimchi, and ice cream. I stood out like a sore thumb and yet, just as I had on my previous travels, I embraced the differences.

On my first day of class, I walked through the main door to Yangjin Middle School and quickly realized that the 1,000+ students zooming by were all staring and giggling at me as I entered the school. I was a redheaded American who was now becoming a part of their school. I had a PowerPoint presentation prepared to show my classes, which basically communicated that I'm American, that I had already been to thirty-nine countries, and that I was in East Asia for the very first time.

Over the course of two years, I became conversational in the Korean language, receiving a black belt in Tae Kwon Do, partying three times a week in Seoul, and traveling to some twenty Asian countries. I also started a travel blog called *The Hungry Partier*. As the name suggests, I wrote about eating and partying around the world—from my previous adventures in Europe to those current trips around Asia. Unlike designing and launching an app, starting a blog only cost eight dollars to register a domain name, and I could hit the ground running.

And so I did. Through my blogging and networking, I discovered a guy named Lee Abbamonte who, at the time, was the "Youngest American to Visit Every Country." He stepped foot in his final country, Libya, at thirty-one years old. There I was as a twenty-three-year-old, with about thirty-nine countries under my belt. I had a new mission: to beat Lee's record. I wanted to visit every country in the entire world, and I would do everything in my power to make that happen.

I've always been the competitive type, growing up playing sports. When I set my mind to something, I am determined to reach my goal, and this new goal was going to be an adventure like few others had taken on. Because whereas other travelers might stop over in a country and consider it visited, I wanted to spend time everywhere I went—and I recommend the same for you. I was going to spend real time in each of the 197 countries, getting to know the culture and people, understanding the beauty and complexities of every nation I toured.

And I was going to share it with the world.

When I left Korea in March 2015, my blog was getting enough traction to earn some revenue through sponsors and affiliate links—around $1,500 a month. While it doesn't sound like a lot, it was enough to cover my travel expenses. My first trip was to India, where I spent three months on a solo backpacking trip. I traveled 2,500 miles from Goa to Delhi, taking trains and buses, sleeping in hostels, and eating street food to save money. But with a stomach that wasn't ready to handle Indian food, I got sick quite a few times, and even worse, I found myself in a fatal bus crash from Udaipur to Jodhpur, which killed two of my fellow passengers. It was one of the most terrifying and tragic experiences I have had on my travels. But like all tragedies, it offered me so many lessons as well.

This life is fragile, and it can be gone in an instant. I knew that day and every day since that I wanted to experience all the world had to offer— and I wanted to experience all of the world.

On April 28, 2015, as I was sitting on the rooftop of my hostel in Jaisalmer, India, looking at the 860-year-old fortress, I discovered Snapchat and began to use it to promote my travels. The more I began to create and share content, the less interested I was in sharing party tips, and the more interested I became in sharing about the people and cultures and communities I was having the chance to meet, creating short videos about the different and diverse countries I was beginning to visit.

I got a massive head start on the platform, before most brands and creators jumped on the bandwagon, and I was able to grow to tens of thousands of followers. All of a sudden, I was collaborating with airlines, tourism boards, and media outlets, creating another income stream to help me travel the world. After India, I went to Eastern Europe to cover all of the countries on the continent that I missed while studying abroad. Finally, I went to Turkey, Egypt, and Georgia before setting off to Bangkok to attend an annual travel blogger conference called TBEX—Travel Blog Exchange.

It was at that conference in 2015 when I met Deanna, who is now my partner, best friend, and love of my life. The first thing I told her was that I wanted to visit every country in the world, and she fully supported my dream. We started traveling together immediately—to her home country of the Philippines, then to Australia, New Zealand, Fiji, Vanuatu, Singapore, and Vietnam. We loved Hanoi so much that we made it our home for six months. On the day we moved in, Deanna gifted me a Canon point-and-shoot camera. She told me that I should start making videos that last longer than twenty-four hours on Snapchat, so I gave it a try. My first video was called "What Can $10 Get You in Hanoi, Vietnam," and within three days it got 100,000 views on Facebook. Soon after, I went to North Korea for three days and made a video there, which racked up ten million views in just a few days.

To many Americans (and even the rest of the world), North Korea is an enigma—a scary, unknown, and dangerous enigma. And here I was, not only traveling there but recording my experiences for all to see.

The moment I saw the figure "10M," I decided it was time to put all my time and energy into making videos. Over the next five years, I decided, I would go on to visit the remaining 130 countries, making a video every day alongside my journeys. By March 2020, I had posted over 1,100 videos across 191 countries, receiving over 2.1 billion views, with only six more countries to go . . . and then the world stopped.

But nothing, not even an international pandemic, would fully stop me from seeing those last six. Because somewhere along the way, hitting that milestone was not just about some crazy goal anymore, it was about understanding how this world works and sharing those adventures with my audience. And that's what I hope to do here with you.

THE THREE Ss

Returning to my old neighborhood in Prague in 2021 gave me a surreal feeling. I walked to the street where I used to live, called Náměstí Míru, threw my arms up in the air, and screamed at the top of my lungs. It was the middle of the day, and everyone was looking at me, but I didn't care. In fact, I barely noticed. Because after ten years, I had just completed my lifelong goal to visit every country in the world by age thirty. I'd visited 197 countries—and it had all started in Prague.

Wait, How Many Countries Are There?

If you Google the question "How many countries are there?" you will quickly realize what a contentious matter this is. The 197 number comes from the 193 UN member states plus Taiwan, Palestine, Kosovo, and Vatican City. I chose those four because out of all the "unrecognized countries" in the world, those four fulfill most qualifications for being considered an independent country: they have their own governments, currencies, passports, flags, and culture.

There are many ways to assess the number of countries, and travelers like me do their best to gauge what is the truest figure. I wouldn't say we're right or wrong, rather that the number is always changing.

From my first day in Prague during my study abroad, I learned the value of being a spontaneous traveler. And it's why I live by the motto JUST GO. I've been wearing those two words across my chest for the last eight years because I strongly believe that life's best moments are found on the most adventurous roads. When we leave what is familiar, we make what once was foreign feel familiar. Prague is where I learned the importance of stepping out of my comfort zone. It's where I learned connection—and how to make important, life-changing, even lifesaving decisions without being able to speak a common language. Prague is where I got my first taste of our beautiful world—and that's why I decided to go back after visiting my final country, Saudi Arabia.

I spent three days walking around Prague without my phone or my camera, smiling from ear to ear as I visited all my old favorite bars and restaurants. I got a tattoo on my arm that says *197*. I couldn't believe it was true. More people have been to outer space than have been to every single country in the world. As of this writing, around 250 in total have done it, and I was one of the youngest—and the only one to finish in the middle of a global pandemic.

Because Prague also taught me something else, even back in 2012. It gave me my ground rules for travel.

> **What I realized is that no matter where you are in the world, you are usually safer than you think, but you're also only as safe as you make it for yourself.**

I wanted to be able to JUST GO, to say yes, but I also have parents (and now a wife) who love me, who I want to return to at the end of every journey.

That's why from that first adventure, I learned the three *Ss*: Be safe, be social, and ALWAYS be spontaneous. I know they sound simple, but you'd be surprised how often a good trip can go bad when people either take too many chances or not enough. Sure, you can go out there and visit a place, go to the museums and the city squares, post your pictures, and come home. Or you can really go out and get to know the world.

Those three *Ss* are something that stick with me everywhere—from the jungles of the Central African Republic to the ski slopes of Argentina to the remote tribes of Papua New Guinea and the brilliant pagodas of Japan. It doesn't matter where I go; these rules have always been ingrained in my style of travel. And honestly, you can travel almost anywhere as long as you're willing to follow them!

This book is organized in parts around those three *Ss*. In these pages, I am inviting you along with me, offering a firsthand look at what it means to visit some of the most exciting, interesting, and dangerous places on Earth. You'll be right there with me as I make hard decisions on what to do and where to go. A huge part of what I do is so that I can bring the world to other people. But I don't show them museums and nightclubs (unless they're really, really fun); I show them what it means to live in the countries I visit. And I don't just share stories of the world so people can watch and read them (though that's cool too). I share them so that others can be inspired to go out there and meet people they've never met before, visit places they've never seen, understand the world as it is—and not how it often gets portrayed on the news or on TV.

It's more than just seeing the world; it's about being a part of it.

When we know where we're going, how to get there, and what to do (and not do) when we arrive, we can experience the incredible and deep connection that exists between everyone on this planet—black, white, brown, Christian, Jew, Muslim. That's why I realized I didn't just want to invite you into my travels, I wanted to show you how you could do them yourself. Does that mean you're going to book the next flight to Baghdad? Probably not. In fact, it's better you don't quite yet. But it does mean you'll be prepared to visit places you never dreamed of going, learning how to travel cheap, safe, and smart so that you can arrive in any country in the world and know that you are home.

To me, traveling is the world's most addictive drug. I get a rush of dopamine every time I meet another person from a different country. I thoroughly enjoy pushing myself outside my comfort zone to try new foods, learn about new cultures, venture to places that few people have seen, and figure out how to use the metro system when I don't know the language.

I live by the motto: "Life begins when you step outside your comfort zone." So, let's step outside; let's step onto the next flight. I can't wait to get on the plane together.

Let's JUST GO!

Be Safe

As cliché as it sounds, the most important thing to consider when it comes to travel is safety. Even though I preach that the world is safer than you think, and 99 percent of people in the world are good people, you must have basic common sense. It's never a good idea to walk down an alley by yourself at three in the morning (even in a safe country like Japan)—nor venture to a district where locals tell you not to go.

PART ONE

📍 Seoul, South Korea

Every country has good and bad people, and the good far outweigh the bad, but that doesn't mean you should get rid of your common sense or take unnecessary risks. In the following chapters, I'll teach you everything I've learned about keeping myself and my stuff safe, no matter where in the world I go.

How to Say "Hello" Around the World

Language | Most common way to say hello | *Pronunciation*

Amharic | Iwi selami newi (እዉ ሰላም ነዉ) |
Ewe-selamee-nuhwee

Arabic | Marhaba (مرحبًا) | *Mur-HAH-ba*

Burmese | Haallo (ဟယ်လို) | *HAAL-oo*

English | Hello | *Heh-low*

Farsi | Salām (سلام) | *Saol-AM*

Filipino | Kumusta | *Koo-moo-stah*

French | Bonjour | *Bon-zhoor*

Hebrew | Shalom שלום | *Sha-lowm*

Indonesian | Halo | *Haw-low*

Korean | Anyeong haseyo (안녕하세요) | *AHN-young-ha-say-yo*

Kurdish | Slav | *Slawv*

Pashto | Salam (سلام) | *Sah-laam*

Portuguese | Olá | *Oh-Laa*

Russian | Privet (Привет) | *Pree-VYEHT*

Samoan | Talofa | *Tah-low-fah*

Spanish | Hola | *Oh-laa*

Swahili | Jambo | *Jam-BOH*

Turkish | Merhaba | *Mer-hah-bah*

Ukrainian | Privit (привіт) | *Pre-veet*

Urdu | Assalāmu Alaykum (السلام علیکم) | *As-salam-u lay-kuhm*

📍 Pyongyang, North Korea

CHAPTER 1

The World Is Safer than You Think (As Long as You Know How to Travel Safely)

I was nineteen years old when I first learned about life in North Korea. I was sitting in a classroom of about eighteen people when our professor played a movie for us, showing how their people lived as brainwashed citizens of a brutal regime—following every move their leader makes. As I watched the North Koreans dancing around to communist propaganda music inside Pyongyang's main square, I thought, *What is this? What is going on?*

The next semester, my curiosity piqued, I presented to the class on the Juche ideology, which is basically the philosophical system that North Korea is based on. I found that North Korea class way more interesting than anything I learned in calculus, physics, English, or Spanish. And because of that, I started teaching myself the Korean language. I studied it on KoreanClass101.com. I took daily lessons. I learned how to read and write Hangul (the Korean script), and I learned how to speak.

And then I had the idea to teach English in Seoul after I graduated.

I knew it would take me closer to North Korea—a goal that I was determined to accomplish. Nobody in that classroom had ever been to

North Korea, including our teacher (who is from South Korea); in fact, nobody I knew had ever been to North Korea.

After college, I moved to Seoul, South Korea, to teach English for two years. And I loved every second of it. I studied the Korean language, immersing myself deeply in Korean culture. I trained to get a black belt, and I partied in Seoul every weekend. I had an absolute blast. Also, I began to discover the similarities and differences between South Korea and North Korea, the inspiration for this adventure.

When it was time to leave my English-teaching job in Seoul, I already wanted to visit every country in the world. And North Korea was one of the 150 that I hadn't yet been to. In many ways, I still can't believe I actually visited North Korea. After the Korean War ended in 1953, South Korea rapidly evolved into the economic, cultural, and tech-savvy hub that it is today—but communist-backed North Korea has since been in isolation from the rest of the world. My grandfather actually fought in the Korean War as a US marine, and he told me some crazy stories about what combat was like against the North Koreans, sharing tales of how his division had to hide out from them and the violence that occurred between both sides. And yet, no one would have expected that seventy years later, North Korea would still be considered our enemy.

It's mind-blowing to think about how life is so normal, uplifting, and technologically advanced in Seoul, but just fifty miles north it is completely the opposite in so many ways. I went to the Demilitarized Zone, the two-mile-thick border between the two Koreas, and I learned a lot about the separation. It's very sad to think that over seventy years ago, thousands of families were split in half and couldn't see each other for the rest of their lives. To this day, they still can't.

North Korea was one of the first countries I knew I would travel to, despite the risks. As an aside, I ended up being one of the last five or so Americans to set foot in that nation.

A few weeks after my trip, travel from America to North Korea was banned largely because of the incident that happened with Otto Warmbier, a tourist from Ohio. You may remember reading Warmbier's story in the news. In 2016, Warmbier was accused of stealing a propaganda poster off the wall of his hotel (coincidentally the same hotel that I stayed at) and sentenced to fifteen years in a labor camp. President Donald Trump directed the State Department to work for Warmbier's release, but he came back home in a coma (it's unclear exactly what happened to him, but medical records indicated he'd been in that state since a month after his sentencing). He passed away in the hospital in Ohio a few days after his release. Right after that, President Trump banned all Americans from entering the communist country, a ban that is still in effect as of this writing.

This is a long way of saying that North Korea might never be on your bucket list—and at this point in time, it probably shouldn't be. Still, the lessons I learned in North Korea have been invaluable for me as I've traveled to other dangerous countries. Because if you can get through North Korea safely, you can get through anywhere. It taught me the basics of tourism safety in high-conflict areas, and if going to a more dangerous part of the world is your goal, this chapter is for you.

First, you'll need to build a team to get you there.

FIND REPUTABLE TOURING COMPANIES

The company that took me to North Korea was called Koryo Tours. It's a British company based out of Beijing, and it was mandatory for all forty-five people on the trip to meet in China's capital for a briefing. They tell you the do's and don'ts (mostly don'ts) that you must follow before entering the country. The three golden rules were (1) Don't disrespect the past or current leaders; (2) Don't take photos of construction (because otherwise it looks like the country isn't perfect); and (3) You MUST bow at the statue of Kim

Jong Il when entering the main square. As for precautions, I just locked up my iPhone and computer in the lockers in the Beijing airport because I was paranoid that they would be taken.

At the time, I had just started making travel videos on Facebook. These were the pre-YouTube days. Right before the trip started, my girlfriend (now wife), Deanna, bought me a video camera and said I should begin documenting my travels. And that kicked off an entire career! I spent three nights and four days in Pyongyang, the capital of North Korea. It was bizarre. It was weird. It was different—but that's what made me absolutely love it.

The moment I boarded that plane from Beijing, I'd never been so nervous in my life. I was so anxious that my palms were sweating. It was a charter flight on Air Koryo, the only North Korean airline. I remember boarding the plane, when I saw North Korean flight attendants, and I was like, *Wow, this is the first time I've seen a human being from North Korea.*

This is ironic because there are twenty-five million people in North Korea, which is a lot of people. It's the fifty-seventh most populous country in the world, yet I'd never seen one human from there. I'm guessing most people reading this book haven't either. Because there is no emigration from North Korea—only people who have escaped.

I hopped on the plane, which was like a 1967 Soviet-built aircraft, and everything was creaky—the wings looked old, and the lights barely worked. It was so nerve-racking, even though it was only about a two-hour flight to Pyongyang, the capital city of North Korea. They served a nasty burger on the plane that was (by far) the most disgusting airplane food I've had in my whole life. It was a cold beef patty that looked like a White Castle burger from hell.

The plane was already bumpy but then we hit a bunch of turbulence, and I became convinced that the plane was going to crash. Not fun. When I closed my eyes, I could see that headline: "North Korea's Air Koryo flight crashes on way to Pyongyang, fifty-five tourists, one American, dead."

And yes, I was the only the American in the group. Most of them were Europeans, Canadians, Australians, and even some Indonesians.

We arrived in North Korea and somehow, some way, the immigration was not that hard because we had pre-approved visas from the tour agency. Thank God. Koryo Tours handles A through Z. All you have to do is pay $2,000 (which is not cheap but well worth the safety measures) and show up in Beijing, and the rest is spoon-fed to you. They book the flights, the hotels, the guides. They get you the visas in advance. They charter the plane. The North Korean immigration officials are briefed on who is coming, which makes it so easy to get inside.

They stamped my passport and then we waited for our bags. And then, BOOM, a "Welcome to North Korea" sign appeared above my head!

> **There is nothing like the rush of going into the unknown—and yes, even the dangerous. But if you're going to a dangerous place, with a safety plan in hand, there is so much to discover about the world—and about yourself.**

If you want to visit North Korea (or any potentially dangerous country for that matter), it's important to do a lot of research and find a reliable tour operator. Read the reviews online, talk to your peers, poke around on social media—and then, use your best judgment and follow the rules.

I know it's easy to dismiss tour companies, since travelers like Otto Warmbier used one, but they can be critical in guiding you through a country where the rules might be different—or bizarre. There is a reason why everyone must attend a mandatory briefing in Beijing the day before the trip: to ensure your safety. And even then, there are some places where even the strongest of protections aren't always enough, as was sadly the case for Warmbier.

A Little Lesson in Passport Privilege

Not all passports are the same. Unfortunately, we can't decide where we are born and which passport we have. I'm very lucky to have a US passport, and I didn't realize that until I started traveling.

Get this: Just because I have that little blue book, I am allowed to visit 186 countries/territories without needing a visa. To put that in perspective, Deanna, my wife, has a Philippine passport, and she can only visit sixty-three countries without a visa.

(If you're from Afghanistan, you're only allowed to visit twenty-six countries without a visa. How unfair is that?)

If you're reading this book and you're American (or Japanese, or from the European Union), then there's a good chance you've never even had to think about visas or apply for one. What's a visa, you ask? A visa is essentially permission granted by the government to enter a specific place or country for a limited amount of time.

There are four kinds of visas that you can apply for, depending on the reason for your trip. There's a tourist visa, business visa, volunteer visa, and a student visa. For me, I've mostly applied for tourist visas. In a few instances, I had a student visa (when I studied abroad in Czech Republic), a business visa (when I taught in South Korea), and one time I had a volunteer visa (which was how I entered Syria—the country was not issuing tourist visas to American citizens at the time).

If you want to check if you need a visa or not, go to the Wikipedia page for your country's passport. A lot of people don't trust Wikipedia as an authoritative resource because anyone can edit it. However, I believe it has its uses, and it's a great way for checking if you need a visa! Simply type in "Passport requirements for ___ (your country) ___ passport." It's always up to date. I've been using it for fifteen years and it's never once failed me. The page will then tell you if you need a visa or not to visit a specific country. If you are not a fan of Wikipedia, or want a backup source, then I recommend Googling the question and reading up on people's responses.

If you are required to get a visa, then the next step is to figure out what kind of visa. There are three options you should know about.

The first is to get an **e-visa** (online). Simply go to whichever country's website to apply, and you are emailed the visa, which you need to print out and show to immigration. An example of a country that requires an e-visa to enter is Turkey.

The next option is to get a **visa on arrival.** Just show up at immigration and then stand in the line that says "Visa on Arrival"—pay the fee, and get your visa stamped in your passport. An example is Ethiopia.

The third is to get your **visa at embassy (apply in advance)**. This is the most tedious and requires a deeper explanation.

Let's use Sudan as an example. If you hold a US passport, then you will need to physically go to the Sudanese embassy in Washington, DC. You have to show up there with all your paperwork, which is usually travel insurance, hotel reservation, a letter of invitation from your host, bank account statements, detailed itinerary, your flight information, and sometimes you have a formal interview. All kinds of fun stuff. Then, if approved, you will be asked to pay the fee (usually by money order or cashier's check, not cash). The price can range anywhere from $100 (the cheapest I've ever paid) to $3,000 (the most I've ever paid), but it's usually between $100 and $300. They will take your passport while they process your application. And then, you have to wait. Sometimes a long time.

Trust me—the wait is the worst part because not having your passport can be really anxiety inducing!

Pro tip #1: If you're American, you can hold two valid US passports at the same time. So, you could travel with one of them while the other one can rack up the visas. If it wasn't for this loophole, then I wouldn't have finished every country so quickly.

If you have a larger budget, you can use a service called Passport Visas Express, where you basically send your passport over to them, fill out all the requirements online, and let them do everything on your behalf. But it doesn't always work for each country, and the price is double or triple to get each visa.

Pro tip #2: You can apply for dual citizenship, which means you could have two (or more) valid passports from different countries. You could have a US passport, and then you can apply for another one due to family background—or simply paying outright. For me, because I'm Jewish, I could apply for an Israeli passport. I could also apply for a Lithuanian passport because my great-grandparents came from there. But if you have money to spend, then you can simply purchase a passport of Paraguay or St. Kitts or a few others for about $120,000. If you are not lucky enough to have a strong passport, then this might be a good option for you, and I know many people who have done it.

START OUT IN PLACES WHERE YOU CAN SPEAK THE LANGUAGE

Finally, after years of dreaming that I would visit this mysterious country, I had arrived. But now what?

Thankfully, I had been preparing for this trip since that day in class when I was nineteen. I knew Korean, and in many ways, North Korea became a different adventure for me because I did.

Because I was able to talk to people and connect with them on a deeper level than just a smile, even when I told them I was an American tourist, and they would just respond, "Oooohhhhh, USA person."

There were about fifty-five of us on the group trip. We all jumped on a white school bus and started driving around. We went to the National Library and museum, which was filled with anti-American propaganda. I mean, videos of bombs going off at the White House, graffiti of the Statue of Liberty on fire, photos of guns pointing at American citizens held hostage. As I was walking through that museum, I thought, *Does the staff here have any clue that I'm American? What would they do if they found out?*

I went through it with an open mind and no facial expression. I wanted to fully embrace it and feel North Korea.

Then our group proceeded to move all around Pyongyang and nearby villages. We went to dinner at the hotel, which was pretty much catered for tourists only. There were no other North Koreans in the restaurant, which was a little bit upsetting. I really wanted to meet North Korean people and immerse myself in their culture.

But finally, I got my first taste of the real North Korea when I took the underground metro. We rode it for eight stops, and we were completely surrounded by North Koreans everywhere. The men had on suits with briefcases in hand, and I didn't know exactly where they were going because I didn't see any hospitals, hotels, or grocery stores, but they were going somewhere.

And that was the first time where I could be side by side with North Koreans and try to smile at them and have them fail to smile back at me. I looked around as people hurriedly left the train, but then once we were in the city, there didn't seem to be any industry or shops.

Everything felt staged. I don't know if you've ever visited a movie studio lot, but it felt like that. There were tall buildings that were completely empty with nothing inside. Fancy gardens outside of buildings and shops, but completely black within.

As I watched people step on and off the train, I thought maybe they were going to school or a sporting event because they're very good athletes. But in terms of jobs, there's nothing.

Even as we drove around the city, it was lifeless. I would watch police-women who were dressed up in head-to-toe uniforms organizing the streets of Pyongyang and the metro traffic, but there were hardly any drivers. Even though I knew Korean, I knew better than to ask any questions.

I discovered early on that if you're in a dangerous situation, the safest thing you can do is sit back and observe, watch the people, learn about your environment, and respect that every culture is different and unique, even if you don't agree with it.

And it's easiest to observe and learn about your environment if you can understand at least a little of what people are saying around you and can ask basic questions (and understand the answers!) if you need to. That's why I think it's important to at least speak a little bit of the language in the country that you are visiting—something like twenty words or phrases goes a long way. And if you only speak one language, such as English, don't forget about the English-speaking nations like Nigeria, Guyana, Ireland, New Zealand, Australia, United Kingdom, and dozens of others.

FIND CONNECTION ANYWHERE

No matter how hard it is to go to a country, there is always a feeling of connection. You will always find a friend. Even in North Korea, I found those people—most notably the hotel staff. Every night, I played ping-pong with them and challenged them to a bowling match. Yes, there was bowling and ping-pong at my hotel. It was like an all-inclusive playground with food, games, activities, and karaoke.

But the highlight of my trip was the day I got to participate in the Pyongyang marathon. I only ran a 10K, but it was the one time on the trip that we didn't have to be with our tour guides. So I freely wandered the streets of Pyongyang and was cheered on by local spectators, who were giving me high fives and words of encouragement.

As I ran through those streets, I was in awe of this mysterious country that somehow managed to keep itself hidden in plain sight. For years, I had dreamed of this moment. After my 10K, I walked the rest of the way, knowing this was the only freedom I would have in a nation that is infamous for its lack of freedom. There were people barbequing along the race route, and I would stop and have a bite and a beer. Though there are always police everywhere, it didn't feel scary, and for the first time, it didn't feel staged. They were only people outside enjoying a beautiful, albeit cold, day, cheering on their friends and family, and tailgating, just like we do back home. And in a way, I was home too.

Anywhere I go, whether it's Spain, Tuvalu, Senegal, or Japan—I feel at home because humans are home, and I can connect with them. I always feel a sense of unity, and a sense of pride, to be able to share these moments with strangers, who then, over food, or laughter, or a cold beer on a cold morning, become friends. And that's the most beautiful thing about travel. That's why I'm addicted to seeing the world. That's why I can't stop exploring.

Sure, the places are cool. But the people are always the real tourist attraction. We'll cover this idea in depth in part two of the book, but I did want to talk about it now.

> **Even the most dangerous countries are full of regular people who are excited to meet you and share about their cultures. This is true from Afghanistan to Zanzibar.**

Although North Koreans seemingly hate Americans (on paper), they are just people who have the same wants and needs as you. They love. They laugh. They cry. And they get excited when meeting strangers. And that's why I urge you to travel because no matter where you go, even a place as different as North Korea, you will always find home.

Unfortunately, my mom doesn't always feel the same way.

DON'T BE AFRAID TO SCARE YOUR PARENTS (OR FRIENDS OR COLLEAGUES OR ANYONE)

My parents are really supportive people; I love them to death. They've always been behind everything I do, and they're really my best friends. But once I started traveling, my mom would always tell me: "Whatever you do, please, do not go to North Korea."

But North Korea is a country, and I had to go.

So, I had to lie. I told my parents that I was going on a camping trip in China, and I would be offline for several days because of no internet. I actually did go to Beijing to attend that mandatory briefing, so the China part wasn't a lie. I called my mom from my hotel in Beijing and said, "I'm about to embark on this camping trip in China and I'll be offline for four days."

Truth be told, I actually left my phone at the Beijing airport because I didn't want the North Korean government to have any way to track me. For someone who works online, it was really hard to do that. It was even more difficult for me to lie to my parents like that. But if I told my mom the truth, she may have convinced me not to go. And to this day, I still would not have been to every country.

So, I went to North Korea and had a blast over three nights and four days. It's the one trip that I think about the most when I reflect on the past ten years of travel.

When I got back to China four days later, I called my mom from the Beijing airport and said, "Mom, I just went to North Korea."

And she said, "You what?" and then hung up the phone, which is the first and only time she's ever hung up on me.

She was crying and she didn't talk to me for a week. She was so mad. My dad, on the other hand, thought it was cool and was asking me questions about it.

But then I got home and began to edit the footage I shot with the camera Deanna gave me. It was the first time I really worked on putting together video footage from a trip, narrating and editing the experience for viewers to see a country from my POV. I put it up on YouTube, and within seven days, my video got ten million views.

And my mom? Well, of course now, years later, she shows all of her friends my videos from North Korea and brags that they have over sixty-five million combined views. Oh, the irony!

But no video can ever replace the memories. And though, at this time, we don't know when another American will get to visit, I think of how little Americans and North Koreans get to know each other, get to meet and talk and go bowling and have a beer, and how, every year that we don't have the opportunity to do that, the less we will remember just how alike we all really are.

What we perceive as dangerous isn't always dangerous. I wouldn't rank North Korea in the top one hundred most dangerous countries in the world. It's actually very safe—as long as you follow the rules—and the truth is, trouble can happen anywhere.

However, from watching the news, my mom believed then—and even more so now—that North Korea is the most dangerous place in the world. If we want to talk Yemen or Somalia or Libya or Syria, she doesn't get as frightened, which is funny, because those countries are literally 10,000 times more dangerous!

But unfortunately for my mom (and maybe yours too since you're reading this book), I love big adventures, and adventure takes risk. The thing about risk is that it can be mitigated—by connecting to the right people, guides, and cultural understandings that can make any place in the world safer than you might think.

📍 Kochi, India

CHAPTER 2

The School of Street Smarts

Wherever you come from—whether it's Los Angeles, Luanda (Angola), or Luxembourg—you are growing up in a bubble.

In your school system, the teachers follow a specific curriculum that is catered to the beliefs of your nation. Your childhood friends (probably) look like you, act like you, talk like you, and most importantly, *think* like you. Many people live their entire life without leaving their hometown, state, or country. While there's nothing wrong with that, it does hinder our ability to be cultured.

I've always believed that you can't understand or appreciate your own country until you travel and experience others and hear what they think about the place you come from—whether that's your town, your state, or your country.

When you travel—to anywhere—you understand how other people live and what they believe in. You learn about new cultures, cuisines, religions, and ideas. And that, inherently, makes you wiser.

Think of your favorite childhood movies—chances are that many of the settings went over your head—but when you travel, and you re-watch those movies, it'll start to click, because you've been to those places. You've understood the cultures, the landmarks, and the people.

Mission: Impossible—Ghost Protocol looks different after you've been to Dubai, just as *Amélie* looks different after you've been to Paris. And I can promise, *Black Hawk Down* became a different experience for me after visiting Somalia. It's one thing to hear about a place or to see it on the internet or TV, but it's another to walk through its streets, meet its people, understand its beauty, and also, see its pain.

I can honestly say that I've learned more from the last ten years of travel than I have from any textbook in school. And the best way to learn is from experience—meeting with people eye to eye and learning about their way of life, and then coming home and sharing what you learned with friends and family and coworkers, passing down your experiences to your kids and your grandkids. Or in my case, on YouTube!

For those in the back, I'll repeat myself again (and probably like a million more times in this book): Traveling is the best education that you can have. You will learn more things from one trip than you can from any article, magazine, or show.

> **Travel helps us step out of our comfort zone, doing things that we wouldn't normally do, and using parts of our brains that we never knew existed.**

At the end of the day, you become smarter and wiser, and that is one of the most beautiful things about travel.

FIND A FRIEND

Before you do anything, make friends. Now, obviously, we'll chat more about this when we talk about being social, but safety begins with who you know. Before any trip, I typically make a post saying, "Hey guys, I'll be in Slovenia, Estonia, and Georgia for the next three weeks, will anyone be around?" And then I get an influx of responses, from which I choose people to hang out with.

For instance, in Venezuela, I met a fellow content creator named Emmanuel, who took me under his wing and let me stay in his house. He guided me across Caracas and escorted me to all the best places in town that would have been impossible to find online. I never had to worry about anything because he grew up in the city, and he knows the best places to go (and not to go).

As long as you're willing to make a human connection (and not just an online connection), you can make a trustworthy local friend! Try striking up a conversation with your hotel concierge or meeting someone at a bar or simply smiling at a person on the street. What about chatting with someone at a restaurant or food stand, or in a store? There are also websites such as MeetUp.com and Couchsurfing.com, and I even started my own app called JUST GO (shameless plug). Because a local friend isn't just someone who can become a future pen pal, they can help to make the most out of your trip. They can speak the local language, they understand the culture, and they know the lay of the land. I always make sure to compensate them for their time (paying for food, gas, activities, etc.), but more often than not, locals just like to show off their countries, cities, and cultures. Think about it—if somebody were to visit your hometown, would you be happy to show them around and make them feel safe? And believe it or not, I have never once been seriously robbed, kidnapped, or mugged—primarily because I'm always with local friends (and my local friends have never robbed me either!).

If you are traveling as a woman, or a member of the LGBTQ+ community, then it's important to take extra precautions to ensure your safety and minimize the risk of getting taken advantage of in some areas. For specific advice on women's travel, I recommend following my friends @EvaZuBeck, @TravelingJackie, and @AnnaEverywhere. And for LGBTQ+ travel, check out @OskarandDan.

Being safe means that you don't let fear stop you from doing what you want to do.

Don't listen to what the news (i.e., the "mainstream media") tells you, because they only share one side of the story—the side that is more viral, more dramatic, and usually earns them more advertising revenue. Trust me when I tell you that it's rarely the same situation when you are on the ground, meeting eye to eye with locals, sharing food, laughter, and jokes. The more you travel, the more you will realize that the world is mostly a safe place.

Physical Safety

No matter who you're with, it's important to pay extra attention to your surroundings. Understand that cities are broken up into different areas, and some of them attract danger. No matter where you go in the world, you can find slums, drug lords (not kidding—there are drug lords literally everywhere), and criminals. So, I advise you to book your lodgings in a safe part of the city. Ask people in your network for their thoughts, read forums online, watch YouTube videos, and educate yourself on the ground as best as you can.

Here are some safety tips to protect you from natural elements:

> Always have sunscreen. The sun is always stronger than you think, even on cloudy days.
> Bring all medications with you for common illnesses, food poisoning, and disease outbreaks. Consult a travel doctor before your trip.
> Always drink bottled water and never eat fresh fruit or vegetables unless you are the one to open, wash, and peel it.

At the end of the day, there can be challenges and dangers any-where you go, from hiking in your hometown to visiting cities on the other side of the world. But if you are able to take basic safety pre-cautions to keep yourself physically safe—and healthy—you will find there is a world out there waiting to be explored and shared.

LEARN LIKE A LOCAL

No matter where you go, one of the best ways to experience the world is to travel like a local! And while you're at it, it's a good idea to avoid the tour-ist traps. I've often had the best food on my travels at the hole-in-the-wall restaurants where locals eat for cheap, not the bigger expensive places in the center of town squares!

When I was in Ecuador, I started my trip in Quito and Guayaquil, the two largest cities—and they were both meh. I was then steered to go to Baños, a tourist town in the center of the country, but I was thrown off by all of the tour packages that they were selling. So instead, I left after a few hours and took a bus down to Cuenca, which was a total game changer! It's my favorite city in the country. It's such a beautiful colonial city, and I didn't see a single tourist while there. It's a completely different vibe than the rest of the cities in the country, and it wasn't on any tourist map.

All I had to do was ask. Once you get to a place, talk to the locals; even if you don't speak the language, you can always use Google to translate the question (and their answer): "If you were visiting your country, where would you go?" And I can promise you, they won't tell you the Eiffel Tower or Times Square. They will tell you of the place you've never heard about, the secrets that make their home so special.

That's what it's all about—going where the locals go. It all comes down to choosing your time wisely.

As you're planning your trip, I recommend you look into local holidays, festivals, or celebrations. There is a holiday in Vietnam called Tết, which marks the first day of the Lunar New Year. It's such a fun time to visit Vietnam because the locals decorate their houses and grab massive trees (think Christmas trees) to bring inside their homes. They transport the trees on the back of their motorbikes by strapping them in, and it's such a unique scene to witness.

Also, look into local independence days for countries. I've randomly visited four or five nations on their independence day, my favorite being El Salvador. What a day it was! The experience of being in the city was so much more enriching because people were marching in the streets with their flags and having the best time with their friends.

Another great one is China during the Chinese New Year! Or the USA during Halloween or Thanksgiving. There are decorations everywhere, music playing, beer bottles opening, and people out and about enjoying life. The one thing about holidays anywhere is that people are usually out celebrating, so you get to meet the locals, experience their customs, and also join in their celebrations. It's an amazing way to see a country, but also a great way to meet the people.

> **The answer is in the locals, to travel like a local, meet locals, and have local experiences. These memories last a lifetime but also, truly, they make us citizens of the world.**

TAKE IT DOWN AND BLEND IN

Look, there's a time and place for the expensive shoes and designer handbags, but I never dress flashy when I travel. I leave my watches, my sunglasses, and my fancy shoes at home (not that I own any). When I'm on the road, I strip down to the basics—a couple of shirts, a few hats, one pair of shoes, and a basic backpack.

The more you flash around your wealth—and no matter how much money you have, being American generally makes you richer than most people in the world—the more likely you are to get robbed. This is especially true when it comes to electronics. One time in Athens, Greece, I was holding a brand-new iPhone 5 (remember those?) in my hand, and it was snatched in front of my eyes (which is why I say I have never been seriously robbed, because most of us have had a cell phone stolen at some point in our lives). So, take it down a notch, keep your fancy duds at home, and your generation 50 iPhone tucked safely away when you're not using it.

Many Americans love to represent their universities or favorite sports teams on their shirts. I was no exception! In my early days of travel, I used to have "The University of Wisconsin-Madison" emblazoned across my chest. But then I got too much unnecessary attention, and I realized that I was at a higher risk of being pickpocketed or having my stuff stolen. So, I learned to try to be incognito and blend in with the crowd. And as a red-headed Jewish guy from Arizona, I have a lot working against me!

That means that very often, I dress like a local. While I don't expect everyone to get so immersed in local cultures, I think it's one of the best possible practices for safe travel.

> **By dressing in local attire, you gain respect from the locals, and you feel safer because you're not standing out from the crowd.**

Think about it this way—you are a guest in someone else's culture, and it's in your best interest to respect them and their customs. If it's forbidden to wear shorts (like it is in many Muslim-majority countries), then, at a minimum, don't wear shorts! It's in your best interest to blend in with the locals, and that's why you'll often see me wearing traditional outfits in countries like Iran, Sudan, or Afghanistan.

HIDE THE CASH

Venezuela was my 194th country—fourth to last. I saved it for the end not by choice, but because the visa was so incredibly hard to get. It was one month before Covid hit, and I had to beg the Venezuelan ambassador at the Manila embassy over a four-week period. Finally, I was awarded the visa, which had a one-year validity, but the country shut down for the ensuing eleven months.

Finally, in February 2021, the country opened its borders, and I was on the very first commercial plane to Caracas. What a thrill it was to be the only tourist in the country. Truly. I was the first foreign national allowed to visit—and the only one on this trip.

Not that there are many tourists any other year. Tourism has been almost nonexistent in Venezuela since the early 2010s due to political instability and a massive economic downfall—twice as severe as the US Great Depression.

It wasn't the first time, but I learned that in countries where there is hyperinflation—meaning the currency in that country could change quickly, it is best to bring a lot of extra US dollars, because you don't know how your own money is going to change value while you're there. But also, don't put it all in one spot. Because if you're in a country with a lot of economic instability, you're likely in a country with a lot of crime.

For Venezuela, I had five different stacks of money, and I kept them in five different places across two backpacks. Because you never know if you're going to get mugged or lose your wallet—you want to have extra cash with you, and US cash is king. Not only is this tip useful for Venezuela but for all over the world—including North Korea. US dollars, not Amex, are truly accepted everywhere.

Another useful lesson that Venezuela taught me was to pay attention to current events and the economic state of any country you visit. Be prepared. For example, in Venezuela, there are no ATMs that accept foreign cards—none. So, you need to be prepared!

Even though I always encourage people to be spontaneous, I still am a strong believer that (at the very least) you need to know the political situations of the country that you're entering. Or else you might have a very hard time!

But no matter where you're going, once you take this little extra time to prepare, you will have the time of your life. Because as I discovered, Venezuela is one of the greatest countries in the world!

As soon as I landed in Caracas and cleared immigration, I was met by my local friend and fellow YouTuber Emmanuel. Over the course of eleven days, he took me around to places that were far off the beaten path like Chuao in the north, an amazing chocolate-producing island with the friendliest locals ever. And we visited this place called Chichiriviche, where we met some local people who invited us inside their house for dinner. I have eaten in mansions, and I have eaten in huts, and I can honestly say that I know the quality and kindness attached to the meal is usually inverse to the size of the home. And it's not that rich people aren't nice, but the humility and openness I have found from people with far less than the rest of us on this planet never fails to overwhelm me. And though we all deserve to be fed and safe, it is such a reminder that the most valuable thing we have is the way we can connect with each other.

I had barely been able to travel that year because of the pandemic, and it was incredible to be on the road again, experiencing this country that has suffered so much in the last decade.

As we drove around, we stopped at little food stands, pulling our car over to take in the beautiful coastline—the largest in all of the Caribbean—and we didn't see a single tourist the entire trip. There is so much hidden value in that! We visited the slums of Caracas, inside "the most dangerous neighborhood" called Petare, which has more killings per year than any other district in South America. But I came out alive, and to be honest, it didn't feel much different than the slums of Mumbai or slums of Manila that I visited. Or even the slums of Los Angeles. Poverty doesn't have a passport. As you will find, it is everywhere—except maybe very few nations such as Kuwait and Iceland.

Believe it or not, Venezuela had one of the most prosperous economies in the world in the 1970s and '80s. It had the highest minimum wage in Latin America and boasted a lot of jobs and a very low unemployment rate. The reason for this was the discovery of oil—the second largest reserve in the world behind Saudi Arabia. But then, in the twenty-first century, things took a turn for the worse. Political instability, economic downfalls, and crazy hyperinflation have completely crashed Venezuela.

When I went there last year, as my 194th country, one US dollar was equal to two million Venezuelan bolívares. Nowadays, just a few years later, that same one US dollar is over five million bolívares. Absolutely absurd.

But despite the failing economy and political system, I learned that Venezuela is still a really beautiful country. They have access to so many things that other countries don't—an abundance of natural resources, the tallest waterfall in the world, historically remote tribes, and of course, the Amazon rainforest. The Venezuelan people are actually a big mix of Europeans, Indigenous, and Africans. I was surprised that the majority of people I met and saw in Venezuela were white skinned—the country is far more diverse than people think. And as my 194th country, I can say that Venezuelans are some of the friendliest people that I've ever met in all my travels—they're outgoing, so fun, and so resilient.

I am telling you now: You will have the time of your life if you ever get the chance to visit, and you'll have stories to share for the rest of your life. It's one of my top ten favorite countries in the world, and I would love to go back sometime soon, so let me know if you're planning to go.

Maybe we can hit the beach together. Just remember to bring cash.

Sometimes, Danger Is in the Eye of the Beholder

Oh, Iraq! Ancient Mesopotamia—the place that you learned about in your first-grade class—is the birthplace of humanity, where the very first settlements began. The exact spot where the Tigris and Euphrates rivers meet, which I visited and loved. Iraq is the place where East meets West. Where ideas, thoughts, and items were spread across the historic Silk Road. I actually visited the world's very first city, called Ur.

And I road-tripped all over the country with my Spanish friend, Alvaro. We went from Baghdad to Babylon, Karbala to Najaf, Samarra to the marshlands—Iraq is beautiful. I even ventured into Iraqi Kurdistan, the northern de facto state of Iraq, where there's so much history and so many smiling faces. It's unfortunate that Iraq has had a bad reputation because of terrorist attacks and extremist ISIS bombings, because the country holds the spirit of our humanity.

Which is why I'm here to tell you that Iraq is fantastic. It's full of life—markets, mosques, and ancient settlements—and though it has had its history of violence, like many places, we often forget about our own country's violence. They have had terrible suicide bombings, but remember that their news informs them of our mass shootings, of which the US had 695 in the year 2022. When I meet people around the world as an American, the first thing they usually say to me is: "What's wrong with you guys and guns?" Many parts of the world are dangerous, but that shouldn't stop us from experiencing them.

BE WILLING TO LEARN

The more I travel, the more I realize how little I know about the world. It's a huge place. There's so much to see and do, and you only scratch the surface when you travel, realizing that there's so much more to be done. And then it's time to pack your bag again.

Travel makes us both book smart and street smart. You become book smart in the sense of learning about history and why certain objects, places, and cultural practices exist. And you become street smart in the sense of connecting with people and figuring out how to get from point A to point B.

Also, you come to understand your true colors and the true colors of the people that you travel with. You are forced to figure out what to do if you get food poisoning. How will you find medicine at a pharmacy, or a doctor at a hospital? How are you going to get around if there's a problem?

For me, that's why I can't stop traveling. To challenge myself. To put myself in situations that I never imagined and figure out how to come out on top.

We learn how far we can push ourselves; the walls of our comfort zone begin to disappear. As I have discovered on my travels to some of the far-thest corners of the world, when you're lying there in the dark, in a foreign land, hearing only the birds calling and the sounds of locals singing, you know that no matter what you might think of yourself, or who you are back at home, you have one thing that no one can take away from you. And that is your humanity.

Travel shows us what it means to be human, and it's the best education that I've ever had. Plus, the greatest part of being human is that there's always more that can be learned.

📍 Yakutsk, Russia

CHAPTER 3

Be Prepared

Preparation is key for any trip, whether you're visiting a country that people consider "safe" or "dangerous"—and I'll be honest, I've had some really dangerous things happen to me in safe countries, and I've had some completely peaceful experiences in some "dangerous" ones. You can never predict the future or know what kind of situations you'll be in. And that's why it's wise to plan ahead to the best of your ability. Some things are easier to prepare for than others, such as visiting the Eiffel Tower, walking on the beach, or going to a restaurant. The only thing that could get in the way to mess up your plans is something bizarre like a natural disaster or if you get sick.

The real challenge comes in preparing for the bad things that *could* happen. What if you get kidnapped? Is there a US embassy (or embassy of your country) nearby? Where is the police station? Who are the best local contacts to have in your phone, should an emergency happen? Not every country has something as simple and convenient as dialing 911—so you must come prepared.

If you don't have safety—or good health—then you have nothing. And once one of those things goes away, you suddenly realize that everything else isn't as important. So being prepared is really essential.

Be Prepared with the Essentials

Here are a few things that you should always have with you when you travel:

> **The phone number and location of your nearest embassy.** Get this information before you go and for every country you plan to or are thinking of visiting. Just in case you lose your mobile connection, write these numbers down in a safe place where you can access them.

> **Travel insurance information.** You should always have travel insurance; World Nomads or Allianz are great options.

> **Extra cash in USD.** It's the most widely accepted currency in the world and can easily be exchanged anywhere. Cash is still king in almost all places in the world.

> **Photocopies of important documents.** More times than not, you'll need more copies of your passport, yellow fever vaccine, or flight tickets, etc. You want to make sure to have it printed and organized.

> **Basic medical supplies.** Going to the doctor while you're traveling is never fun. Of course, sometimes you can't avoid it (if you get hurt or get sick), but you can avoid needless doctor visits by traveling with your own medicine bag. You know what you might need. If you regularly use a pain reliever or allergy medicine at home, take some with you.

> **A traveler's wardrobe.** When it comes to clothing, you don't need much. As I always say, "Pack twice the money and half the clothes." You don't need fancy clothing (see "Take It Down and Blend In" on page 24 and my packing list on page 50). If you need something on the road, you can always buy it!

Of course, if you are traveling to a cold climate, then you will need to add a lot of warm layers. If you are traveling for long enough and need to do laundry, find a laundromat. You can always find a laundromat for two to five US dollars at any given place, and it's super easy to just do a load. I don't recommend laundry services in hotels; they are overpriced.

> **A bunch of locks!** They are your best friends. You can use them for keeping your bags secure from other travelers (at hostels) or from the cleaning staff (at hotels). Or just potential thieves in general.

BE PREPARED FOR BRIBERY

We need to talk about Kazakhstan. I went to Kazakhstan solo for four days in 2017. It was in early March, and I hadn't felt temperatures that cold in many years. It was –25°F.

One afternoon, I was taking a stroll along the main street in Astana, taking photos of a local monument. A policeman came by in his big Soviet-looking puffy hat, said some condescending words in Russian, and then threw me in his police car. I had no idea that I was doing anything wrong, but apparently, you can't take photos or videos of monuments. Thankfully, I knew about thirty or forty words in Russian, which I had studied leading up to this trip.

He asked for my passport, and I told him in broken Russian that I left it at my hotel, which was a one-minute walk away.

"I'm taking you to the police station," he said in Russian while pointing to his badge—which I understood by context and my very limited knowledge of the Russian language.

Now, I'll stop us here. Kazakhstan is actually a pretty safe country to visit (in terms of getting pickpocketed, mugged, or kidnapped); however, it's a former Soviet country which gained independence in 1991, and that means a strict set of laws are still in place. Many people over the age of forty-five grew up during communist times and still have that same mentality. Because of this, there is nothing more intimidating than their police.

But in this moment, I knew how I could get out of it because I prepared for a situation like this. Bribery.

While bribery is illegal in the US and many other Western countries, it's a standard in other parts of the world. In some places, like Kazakhstan, bribery is baked into its culture.

So, while I sat there in the passenger seat of the cop car, I took off my glove, reached into my pocket to grab my wallet, and offered him 14,000 Kazakh tenge (thirty dollars). He immediately took it, gave me a nod of approval, and pointed at my window, which I understood to mean *get the fuck out right now.*

Traveling safe doesn't mean you won't encounter dangerous moments, but being prepared will help you to navigate those moments safely.

Lesson learned—do not photograph any building or monument in Kazakhstan (as well as other former Soviet countries). Had I been more prepared that this was off-limits to shoot, I would have been able to mitigate this disaster. But it happened, and you live, and you learn. And sometimes, you learn to bribe.

BE PREPARED FOR CRIME

This is perhaps my scariest travel story, and it was partially avoidable if I had been more aware of the customs around taking photos (this time of people, not of monuments).

Chad is a tough place to visit in general, and you can immediately see this by the huge UN presence in the capital city of N'Djamena. For years, there has been a significant amount of political instability and turmoil, and I went there all by myself. I met a local person, let's call him Nick. He's six foot eight and was a friend of a friend through an Instagram follower. Together we embarked on an adventure around town together.

Nick was a nice guy. He met me in my hotel lobby and was quick to sit down and make me feel comfortable. He invited me to a restaurant on the other side of town, and to get there, we had to take a motorbike taxi (these are popular in Chad and around Central Africa). We each got on a separate motorbike and were on our way.

I hadn't gotten a local SIM card yet, so my phone wasn't working, but somehow, I felt comfortable knowing that Nick was with me . . . until he wasn't.

My driver sped up through the dirt roads, running red lights, and before I knew it, I was caught in a full-blown police chase. Nick was nowhere to be found, and my phone didn't work. I screamed at my driver, "STOP RIGHT NOW," while patting his back with force, but he responded, "NO," and continued speeding up. Dirt was kicking up in our faces, and horns were honking at us as we just barely dodged cars. It was like when you watch a car chase in a movie, and you think: *no one would survive that.*

Except I was in the car chase, and I was pretty sure I wasn't going to survive it. It was the scariest moment of my life.

Finally, the dust settled, and we stopped at an intersection. I jumped off the bike and I saw five cops running at full speed toward my driver. A brawl occurred right in front of my eyes.

It turns out that my "taxi driver" was not a taxi driver. He was a criminal who had stolen the bike that we were riding on, and the cops were after him.

I ducked out of the scene and jumped into a small, shared bus. I had no idea where I was, no idea where Nick was, and I had no working phone signal. But I did have my camera in my hand, and if you know me, you know I love to document everything that I can.

While in the shared bus, I was filming myself and then turned the camera on a young kid who was looking at me. This was a mistake that I could have avoided if I knew that it's frowned upon to film others in Chad. I was yelled at by everyone in the bus—so much so that I had to jump out at the next stop. That led to another brawl in the street, except this time, I was the person in the middle of the circle, as a bunch of locals surrounded me.

Some of the angry men grabbed my shirt by the neck, and one guy took out a knife. I was already running on so much adrenaline, I didn't know what would happen next.

Out of fate, Nick showed up (he had been looking for me the entire time) and got in between me and the angry guys to calm them down, explaining that I didn't understand what was happening.

"What are you guys doing? He's a tourist! Leave him alone!" Nick screamed in French.

Nobody around spoke English, just French and their native tribal languages.

"Please leave me alone! I am innocent, I'm not trying to hurt anyone!" I said frantically. I really was scared for my life, and after fifteen minutes of scuffling, Nick managed to calm everyone down.

Lesson learned: don't ever separate from a local friend in a country where you can't speak the language.

I went back to my hotel and, admittedly, I changed my flight to leave Chad the next day.

Looking back, I will admit that I was just in the wrong place at the wrong time for the motorbike incident. But I could have been more prepared if my phone worked and I mapped out where my hotel was and where the restaurant was and I had Nick's number. Also, maybe it would have been a better idea to take a taxi than a motorbike.

As for the incident on the bus, well, I have nobody to blame but myself. It's my fault that I photographed the little kid. Had I been more prepared on the cultural etiquette of Chad, I wouldn't have done it, and I might have been able to spend more time in Chad to see and get to know the people.

I'll say that I had some regret leaving. Unlike other travelers, I don't visit countries for the stamp, I visit for the people and cultures, to find out what lies beneath the stereotypes and scary stories. But I also know we have to honor our intuitions, and I've been traveling for long enough to know that if a place doesn't feel safe, there is no reason to stay. Ego, pride, and being tough don't mean anything if you're dead.

Even though I might have betrayed my mom by going to North Korea, I try to think of her, and my wife, Deanna, when I travel. Are they going to care that I left someplace early—or that I came home safe?

BE PREPARED FOR SCAMS

The island of Papua is split into two nations—Indonesia and Papua New Guinea. I went to the Indonesian side on a mission to visit the Korowai people, who are primarily known for being one of the world's last cannibal tribes. It's a story that I'd wanted to explore for years, and I was stoked to finally have the opportunity to tell it, even if I was very nervous to meet a cannibal tribe.

And I'm sure this will come as no surprise, but the trip was wild.

The tribe lives scattered in the middle of the Papuan jungle. They survive completely off the land, hunting for fish in the stream, eating the tree bark (called "sago"), and living a very humble lifestyle out in nature. They have little contact with outsiders.

To get there, I met up with a friend of a friend of a friend, a guy named Otis, who was a nice guy, but didn't speak English very well. He helped me navigate around town and find a local guide who could take me into the tribe, because Otis had no experience going there himself.

After two days of running around the city of Jayapura, looking for a guide, we managed to find a guy named Martin. I filmed our negotiation on my phone. We agreed on the price of $500 USD, which would cover guiding me through the jungle, all meals, and a local driver. The next day, Otis, Martin, and I took a domestic flight to the jungle to spend forty-eight hours living with the tribe. Upon arrival, I learned we were actually visiting the Momuna, which is a sister tribe of the Korowai, but I decided to stay to learn more about their lifestyle. Martin ended up not being a really solid guide—and he didn't even help with anything once we got to the tribe. He just chilled there and cooked while I was out exploring. Still, I was able to film one of the most surreal stories of my life, learning about the tribes' ancient traditions, following them into the jungle to go hunting for shrimp and bobcats, and sitting by the fire to speak with them. Through an English-speaking local named Carlos, some of the Momuna told me that the Korowai tribe still practices cannibalism, though they do not eat people for nutritional benefits but rather as a form of punishment (for example, if you steal or cheat, you will be killed and eaten to remove the demon from your spirit). After spending a few days with the Momuna, I realized that at the end of the day, we are all human, separated by some customs and united in many others.

Though I'd been nervous about meeting a cannibal tribe, as I discovered, it wasn't cannibals I needed to be afraid of. At the end of the trip, not only had Martin been unhelpful with the expedition, but he claimed that there was a miscommunication and demanded that I pay him $1,000 total or I would not be able to fly back to Jayapura. What the hell!! Why would I pay him $1,000 when he didn't do what he'd promised? I really hate being in these situations, especially when I'm not with a friend or a camera guy and nobody is on my side.

Martin was yelling at me while we were standing outside the airport, but I managed to stay calm and hold my ground and did not pay him the $1,000. I got on that flight back to Jayapura with a big sigh of relief. But the story doesn't end there. Martin had contacted the local police in a nearby town and made up some story that I committed a crime and was on the loose in Jayapura. The police called my phone five times, but I didn't pick up because I didn't recognize the number. Otis called me and said that the police were after me and that I needed to be careful not to be captured at the airport.

> **There are going to be moments when things will get scary—especially as you go to more remote and unknown places—but keeping your calm is the best thing you can do, no matter what challenges or threats you might be facing.**

I got out, obviously, as I am here telling you the story. But I'm sharing this because even after visiting 197 countries, I was still being reminded of how important it is to be prepared. If I had been prepared to be with an English-speaking local friend, the rest of the trip would have been easily avoidable. It's why it's so important to have a trusted partner on your big adventures—someone who could help translate anything and help navigate these tough situations where a lot can get lost in translation and bad actors might want to take advantage of a Western tourist.

Now, ninety-nine times out of one hundred, you won't even have to worry because things will go smoothly!

But the more you prepare for a disaster to happen, and the more experience you have with traveling, the better you will be at controlling your emotions and managing the situation in the rare instances when things go south. It's always fear of the unknown that clogs our minds. If shit hits the fan, you can have more comfort knowing that you already thought everything through, and you have a plan of attack. My best advice is to think about all the potential things that could go wrong before you travel—such as losing your passport, becoming sick or injured, getting pickpocketed, losing your wallet or phone, getting lost with no help, jumping in a sketchy taxi cab, etc.—and write them down on paper or in your iPhone notebook.

Spend time playing the tape through: How would you handle any potential challenges or dangers, and who would you have to call? Think about how you would get out of any tough situation and make a plan in advance.

The more you prepare your body and your mind, the more you will be prepared for when these hypothetical situations become a reality.

And the more you travel, the more tough situations will arise. Those are just the stats of life.

Panicking is the worst thing that you can do. The more you prepare yourself, the more you'll appreciate and enjoy the journey!

♥ Uttar Pradesh, India | Riding a bike across Uttar Pradesh, a state in northern India that borders Nepal. I was heading to the city of Rishikesh, which sits on the foothills of the Himalayas.

♥ Hong Kong, China | Looking at the best view over Hong Kong from Victoria Peak. With an elevation of 552 meters (1,811 feet), it's the tallest hill on Hong Kong Island.

Karachi, Pakistan | Filming outside a busy market. Karachi is the biggest city in Pakistan and has tons of markets where you can buy pretty much everything from new electronics to antiques.

Dhaka, Bangladesh | Gazing at the monuments in Dhaka. This three-domed mosque was part of a series of buildings constructed at Lalbagh Fort. Lalbagh means "Red Garden" and also refers to that style of reddish and pinkish architecture.

📍 **Fereydunshahr, Iran** | Would you believe me if I told you the best skiing I've done was in Iran? Yes, it snows in Iran, and it snows a lot! I had a blast spending a snowy day with my local friend and tour guide, Amin—we skied down every mountain on the slopes in the morning, and then by late afternoon, I was playing 18 holes of golf at the best course in the country. Iran is truly a country of wonders!

📍 **Machu Picchu, Peru** | After trekking many miles, I made it to one of the most mysterious ancient settlements called Machu Picchu, set high in the Andes mountains. Can you believe that this dates back to the early 15th century?

📍 **Pyongyang, North Korea** | Making some memories of the view from my hotel window. The Taedong River flows through the city of Pyongyang, which is located close to the mouth of the river on the Yellow Sea.

📍 **Moscow, Russia** | Near the Cathedral of Saint Vasily the Blessed, commonly known as St. Basil's Cathedral. Its architectural style is unlike anything else in the world.

📍 **Greenland** | After cruising for four days through the world's largest and northernmost national park (Northeast Greenland National Park), we made it to the eastern shores of Greenland. And it was spectacular! Fewer than 60,000 people live on this massive island.

📍 **Pyongyang, North Korea** | Running in the Pyongyang International Marathon was an experience I'll never forget. Tourists can enter, and you can run a marathon, half marathon, 10k, or 5k.

📍 **Milan, Italy** | Our pug, Dudoy, is also an accomplished international traveler!

📍 **Jodhpur, India** | Located in the Thar Desert, the walled city of Jodhpur is known as the Blue City because so many of the buildings are painted this iconic blue color.

📍 **Éfaté, Vanuatu** | Teaching some of the locals how to use Snapchat in a small village on the island of Efate.

📍 Prague, Czech Republic | Prague is my favorite place in the world—where it all started! Staroměstské náměstí, or Old Town Square, was founded way back in the twelfth century.

📍 Somewhere in Mauritania | The daytime view on the iron ore train. I wonder how many tons of iron ore you can see in just this picture alone, which captures only a short segment of the train—the longest and heaviest in the world!

📍 **Ubud, Bali, Indonesia** | The rice terraces in Ubud are an incredible destination in Bali and a UNESCO World Heritage Site. Local rice farmers work these cascading fields.

📍 **Antarctic peninsula** | Okay, so, Antarctica is a continent and not a country, but we still considered it an unmissable destination. Fun fact: the Antarctic Ice Sheet is the largest single piece of ice on Earth.

📍 Sahara Desert, Mauritania

CHAPTER 4

Take the Risk—If It's Worth It

Sometimes, it pays to live dangerously.

In the West African country of Mauritania, there is a train. Not just any train. It's both the longest and heaviest train in the world. But this train is not for passengers; in fact, it has only a few humans on it. This train is an iron train, carrying thousands of tons of iron ore in open cars across the Sahara Desert daily, from the iron mines of Zouérat in the north, through Choum, all the way to the beach town of Nouadhibou on the western coast. While it's technically illegal to ride it, the police turn a blind eye to the fact that many locals (and adventure seekers like us!) hitch a ride by literally jumping on as it passes through the country.

One of my friends had jumped on the train a few years before I did, and since then, it had been on my bucket list for nothing more than the pure adrenaline rush.

So my content creator friend Thomas and I decided to do it. But making the decision was the easy part.

EVERY BIG ADVENTURE STARTS WITH LOGISTICS

Big adventures often take big-time planning. What methods of transportation are you going to take to get to your desired destination? How much will it cost? How much cash do you need on hand? Will you need a translator to join you? What kind of food should you bring? What kind of first aid equipment might you have to pack in your bag?

Planning the iron ore train was stressful . . . especially because there wasn't much information online about it, which meant we were going to have to figure out a lot of things once we got there! My friend Thomas and I only planned our flight into Nouakchott, Mauritania's capital, and the rest we had to figure out when we arrived, because there are (understandably) no tour agencies that will help you illegally jump on a train. There was no English spoken whatsoever. Not that that's a bad thing in and of itself; I usually enjoy trying to communicate with emotion and (made-up) sign language, and it always works—but this time, we had business to take care of. Thankfully, Thomas speaks fluent French, which is (along with Arabic) one of the nationally recognized languages in Mauritania. So he was able to find a place for us to sleep, help locate the best restaurants, speak with random taxi drivers for directions, and even make some local friends for us!

As you know, and as we'll talk about in the next part of this book, I'm a big proponent of having local friends to help you, but in certain places it's almost impossible to get in touch with locals until you're there. Luckily, we managed to find a friend of a friend, Muhammad, whose father, Abdul, offered to let us crash at his house and cooked us delicious Mauritanian meals. Abdul told us that he knew a taxi driver who could take us to Choum . . . a seven-hour drive away.

Eventually, we got to Choum. Choum is kind of a run-down, sandy, dusty place. It is a very simple desert town. And we were probably the rare tourists. We showed up in the town, and our driver announced, "Okay, here we are in the middle of the city." But there wasn't much to be seen. A laundromat, an apartment complex. No hotels (and definitely nothing you could find on Airbnb or Booking.com). There was a small bed-and-breakfast, which was run out of a local store, but the bed was literally a little mat in the middle of the shop. On the floor. In the corner, there was an ancient TV with a flickering screen. The room was really dirty. Flies everywhere. Thomas and I looked at each other and put our stuff down, looked at each other again, and said, "We can't sleep here."

We knew if we tried, we wouldn't get any rest! And we had a wild ride ahead of us.

So, we asked around. Finally, we found another apartment complex. And we found a guy who said, "Oh, I know a friend. You could stay in his apartment for twenty-five dollars US a night." (As it turned out, the apartment had satellite TV, and we watched a bunch of movies that night, like *Home Alone*. What a fun memory.) All we knew was that in the morning, the train would leave from the mine, which was a twenty-minute drive away. And when the train arrives at the mine, it doesn't wait for passengers. It stops for sixty seconds and then proceeds along its route.

So, we woke up early the next morning to be ready. The guy whose house we had stayed in told us that the train was supposed to leave at noon. We had to stop and get baguettes, bananas, and water bottles to bring with us on the nineteen-hour journey. There was not much else to do in Choum but go to a market. There were no other stores or cafés. We packed the food we bought in pillowcases because it was easy to transport and would keep our food clean from dirt and dust.

We arrived at the mine at 11 AM, covered from head to toe in local Mauritanian clothes, a blue dress with a white turban. And then we waited in the blistering hot sun. The hours ticked by: 1 PM, 2 PM, 3 PM, 4 PM. Finally, after five hours of waiting, we decided to take a nap in a little hut by the tracks. Nobody was around.

The train finally arrived around 6 PM and, as we'd been warned, we had one minute to throw our backpacks and pillowcases of food into an open train car that was filled to the brim with iron ore. We were exposed to the elements with nothing but sand dunes and camels around us, sitting on top of the iron ore that was stacked at least ten feet high in our train compartment. It was equally as beautiful as it was terrifying. We had to figure out how to assemble our home for the next day, scrambling in the ore just to be able to lie down horizontally (my back has never hurt so much as it did after that). The iron ore piles up high, and it's like clunky sand on a beach, so you have to lie down flat to be able to stay above it and try to remain comfortable—or as comfortable as you can, lying down on tons of iron ore.

The ride was dark for the first twelve hours. The train passes at one point through the unrecognized country of Western Sahara, which is really cool—it's a disputed territory in the north and west of Africa, and as an unrecognized country it's not one of the 197 areas on my list, which only makes me want to visit it more. I don't count going through it as visiting, because we never got off the train (kind of like I don't count an airport layover as visiting).

At night, it was very cold (around thirty degrees Fahrenheit), and we huddled in our sleeping bags. Whenever we had to pee, we'd go in a water bottle. (Thankfully, neither of us had to go number two. Otherwise, we would have done it in a bag and thrown it over the edge.)

As we lay on top of the train, the day receding into night over our heads, the Milky Way was purple, stretching all across the sky. We barely slept but it didn't matter; we were having one of the most incredible out-of-body experiences of our lives—being way out in the Sahara desert by ourselves and feeling the power of nature. It was as if we were actors in a thriller movie, but this was the peaceful scene before the action happened, just the two of us lying out under the night sky, in awe of this adventure we had embarked upon.

This was the reason for all the hard work of these big adventures, experiencing parts of the world few others have or will.

The next morning, we woke up to the most beautiful sunrise over the Sahara. As the sun came up over the desert, Thomas and I broke off pieces of our bread. We were covered in iron ore, our faces black under our turbans. We sat there watching the sun burn along the desert, the light stretching out toward us, and the now-stale baguettes tasting like the greatest meal on Earth.

"Bro, are you feeling what I'm feeling?" screamed Thomas, as I could barely hear him over the noise of the train.

"I am high on life right now," I yelled back. "This is a freaking dream come true."

"For real, dude. And this bread is everything!" he hollered.

My brand name is JUST GO, and Thomas's is SEEK DISCOMFORT, and each of us was wearing our shirts. So we sat there and had a moment of JUST GO, SEEK DISCOMFORT.

Though the trip was wild, with the heat of the day climbing to near one hundred degrees Fahrenheit, the desert was peaceful, reminding us both how long it has endured across the continent and how untouched it still is. Like the little town of Choum, there is no reason for people to come into the deep desert and change it. As skyscrapers rise up across the world, and the developing nations get more developed, it is always amazing to see what stays raw, the parts of this world that never change.

We had made it through the long, cold night on the train, and as we approached Nouadhibou, I realized how easy it sometimes is to scare ourselves out of the big adventure. We think of everything that can go wrong, but then when we're in it, it feels far less dangerous.

When we got to Nouadhibou, we snuck off the train without anyone seeing, as there are only train engineers and no conductors. I had the biggest smile on my face. We walked with our bags to a café to wash our faces and it was just the most . . . I've never been so dirty, and I've never been more thankful to get a cup of coffee and a croissant to eat. That was the biggest taste of victory I think I've ever had in my entire life.

Everything You Need in Two Backpacks

Before I go on any trip, I have a little packing checklist on my iPhone that I look through to make sure my backpacks are packed accordingly. Aside from the normal stuff like clothes, toiletries, and hats, I spend extra time double-checking the important things like electronics, my backup iPhone, both of my SIM cards (one is T-Mobile and the other is Google Fi), my hotel reservations, visas, passport, local contacts, etc. Here's a quick list of everything in my two backpacks.

BIG BACKPACK | *Osprey 40L Porter series*

- Drone—Mavic Air 2
- Dopp kit (I have a dopp kit with a "hanger thing" so I can hang it in the bathroom and then open it up and put it on the wall.)
  - Dental floss
  - Toenail clipper
  - Shaver
  - Toothpaste
  - Toothbrush
  - Shaving cream
  - Face lotion
  - Haircut buzzer
- Electronics bag
  - A bunch of extra hard drives
  - Batteries
  - Earphones
  - Cords
- Clothes (I'm a minimalist and I pride myself on it!)
  - Four different colors of my JUST GO shirts
  - A long-sleeved shirt
  - One pair khaki multipurpose pants
  - Two pairs shorts (one khaki, one dark)
- Four pairs of underwear
- Four pairs of socks
- Hat
- Medicine Pouch
  - Pills for stomach
  - Tape
  - Extra toothpaste
  - Azithromycin
  - Ciprofloxacin
  - Pepto Bismol
- Side pockets of my bag
  - Belt
  - Headlight (blackout, camping, or sleeping outside)
  - Extra filters for camera
  - Extra microphones
  - Microfiber towels
  - Sharpies, extra accessories
  - Emergency compressed cotton towel
- Top part of the bag (easily accessible stuff)
  - Deodorant
  - Golf balls (I play a lot)
  - ChapStick (from the actual ChapStick company)
  - Mosquito spray
  - Locks

- ○ **Front portion of the bag**
  - ○ Collections from around the world: souvenirs (flags, maps, airplane tickets)
  - ○ Masks
  - ○ More medicine
  - ○ Extra money in US cash
  - ○ Pens
  - ○ Ziplock bags—very important!
  - ○ Backup iPhone
  - ○ Local currency
- ○ **Back part of the bag**
  - ○ Important documents (visa requirements, flight tickets, insurance, copies of passports, Covid tests)
  - ○ My "safe," which is a ziplock bag w/ most important stuff
- ○ Yellow fever card—mostly needed in African countries, showing that you have been vaccinated for yellow fever
- ○ Covid vaccine card
- ○ All SIM cards from around the world
- ○ Credit cards that I'm not using in my wallet
- ○ Business cards
- ○ Passport photos in different sizes (because sometimes you need them for visas on the road)
- ○ Scuba diving license
- ○ Backup memory cards

MY SMALLER BACKPACK | *(mostly for electronics/valuables)*

- ○ **Sony a7S III camera with two lenses**
- ○ **MacBook Pro 13"**
- ○ **MacBook charger**
- ○ **Phone and camera chargers**
- ○ **Batteries**
- ○ **Little pouch with all the extra wires and cords that can be plugged into the computer**
- ○ **Sneaky pouch to keep extra US dollars**
- ○ **Memory cards**
- ○ **2 TB hard drive**
- ○ **Memory card wallet**
- ○ **One-meter/three-foot phone charger cord**

For the last ten years, I've been able to use this system of two backpacks and never EVER pay to check my bag under the plane. This system isn't for everyone, but if you can pull it off, it will save you a lot of time, money, and stress!

So there you have it—the basics you'll need to be prepared for safe and seamless travel. But then there's the stuff you really can't plan for. ∎

This is what adventure is all about. Stepping out of your comfort zone and knowing that you've just done one of the craziest things that you could possibly do in the world, even crazier than skydiving or bungee jumping or other daredevil activities. It was worth every second of the experience, and I'd do it again in a heartbeat.

I think about that train ride across the Sahara every day. Not just because it was so memorable (even though it was). But because my AirPods case still has iron ore stuck in it. I don't plan on ever cleaning it out.

TAKE PRECAUTIONS

As much as I preach the value of spontaneity (as we'll explore in part three), there is a time and place for extra planning. And Yemen is one of those places.

Yemen is without a doubt the most dangerous country in the world for a variety of reasons: the ongoing civil war, the turmoil, the chaos, the political unrest, the instability, not to mention the terrorist groups such as al-Qaeda that have been running the country for years. The country has been off-limits to tourism since 2014, with the main airports being shut down along with most land borders. Very few outsiders have been able to get inside unless they can show a Yemeni passport.

But there are loopholes, and I wanted to take the risk to go there (A) because I was going to every country in the world, and Yemen is a country; (B) because of its beautiful, rich, ancient history that I heard so much about; and (C) to be able to film it and share the reality of its people on YouTube. Yemen has fascinated me for years, mainly for its interesting Jewish identity, which is a different sect of Judaism that isn't practiced in other parts of the world. Believe it or not, more than 100,000 Jews in the world are of Yemeni descent, with only fifty families left behind inside of Yemen itself.

Truth is that I really enjoy being the messenger; I want to film these faraway places and share the best of this world—and the best of humanity.

I'm passionate about telling stories in countries that people are too scared to visit.

But Yemen is another beast.

I was so nervous to visit Yemen. I took a massive risk by going alone (mostly because I couldn't find anyone to join me). No camera guys, no friends, no significant others, no acquaintances. So much could go wrong. I'd heard so many things about terrorism and kidnappings and chaos. As a disclaimer, even today I do not encourage any traveler to go to Yemen without professional support. It is not a place for amateur travel. But I felt that I was experienced enough to take the leap. I knew the potential risk and repercussions of going there. I looked at it as high risk/high reward, so off I went to uncover one of the world's most closed-off countries.

I did (eventually) have a local tour guide, Abdul, who I would meet at the land border between Oman and Yemen. I got in touch with Abdul through my Spanish friend, Alvaro, who has also visited every country and told me about him.

I also had to plan—more logistics. I do try my best to stay away from online articles and random news sources, because I believe that what you hear on the news will mislead you about the true nature of many countries. But I couldn't stay away from it for Yemen. I needed to know which areas were controlled by al-Qaeda and which areas were okay to visit. Nobody else that I knew had ever gone to *mainland* Yemen; most of the "every country" travelers go to Socotra, an island off the southern coast, to check Yemen off their list.

I learned that only the Hadhramaut state in southeastern Yemen was available to visit only if you have the proper letter of invitation, and to get there, you had to cross the land border from Oman. Yemen's capital city of Sana'a, as well as the big port city of Aden, were both off-limits and impossible to reach. The Iranian Houthis (rebels) were controlling the regions that host those cities, and I would absolutely get kidnapped or held hostage if they saw an American coming in by land.

I had to find an expert who knew Yemen—but I failed to find any until Alvaro introduced me to Abdul. I did have several Yemeni-American friends/contacts, but I needed someone who was on the ground and who knew the current situation. I chose not to contact the US embassy, even though a lot of people in my situation would have, and the reason was I didn't want them trying to stop me or to talk me out of the trip. I wrote down the number of the embassy and gave it to my wife and friends and family, should there be any problems. But I decided not to contact them unless I was in an emergency situation.

I did make a detailed plan/itinerary based off my own research, to the best of my ability. I included where I would be going, where I'd be staying, and what would be going on. It was challenging to do this without any response from Abdul (before the trip), but I did my best.

To begin the trip, I flew into Salalah, Oman—a city in the southwestern part of the country, which is really far away from the capital of Muscat. Abdul had arranged for a driver to meet me at the airport with my name on a sign, and I had no problem locating him. The driver didn't speak a lick of English, but confidently guided me into his car to start the three-hour journey to the Oman/Yemen border.

This part of Oman is green and tropical—not a desert—and as we drove through the countryside, it was hard to believe that we were headed to such a dry and arid place as Yemen! Of course, my phone didn't work because my T-Mobile plan didn't cover this part of the world. Go figure. We proceeded to drive through amazing mountain ranges, valleys, and green forests where birds were chirping, and dolphins were swimming in the ocean. It was incredible!

Finally, we got to the border, and there was no gate, only a slim rope string with a Yemeni flag hanging from it, as if someone put it together at the last minute. The border office, which was smaller than a small closet, contained a man sitting behind a tiny makeshift desk. I had my little letter of invitation to enter Yemen, which I took out and presented to the immigration officer. There were two guards there with big guns strapped to their chests. One asked, "Are you going to Yemen?"

"Yes," I said.

"Show me your letter of invitation."

I showed them. The agent asked, "Where's your local friend?"

I said he was waiting for me over the border (which he was supposed to be doing).

"No, you cannot enter without your friend," the customs agent replied.

I managed to convince him that I would be safe with my driver, and we would be meeting my guide, Abdul, in the first town across the border. (Remember what I said about my phone? I couldn't call Abdul—still no signal.)

"Go," they said and moved the rope away for my driver to drive inside.

We had just entered Yemen, my 171st country.

We drove for a few minutes, but there was no sign of Abdul. I was pissed. I debated if I should just turn back or if I should continue going. But ultimately, I decided to trust my gut and continue. En route, my driver took me to some guy's house off the main road, where we ate chapati and lamb and rice. Even though I felt safe in that house, I was scared that Abdul wasn't there. What if I was being set up? What if I was about to be kidnapped?

My phone didn't work. I was in the most dangerous country in the world. What the hell!

Finally, Abdul rang my driver. I grabbed the phone and yelled, "ABDUL, WHERE ARE YOU, MAN?"

"Sorry, bro . . . I got a flat tire. We will meet in the next town."

Those were not the words I wanted to hear.

At that point, I was really considering going back to the border and into Oman. The problem was that there were no taxis in Yemen, or at least in this part of the country, and my driver was not going to turn back because he needed to get to his family in Yemen. The place was very run down with dirt roads and no streetlights. I wasn't going to hitchhike back to Oman. So, I was kind of stuck. I had to put my full trust in Abdul that we would indeed meet in the next town.

After a one-hour anxious drive, we made it to Al Ghaydah as soon as it turned dark. And sure enough, when we got to my hotel, a guy came running at me, speaking English. "Hello, Drew! You made it!"

"Hi, Abdul," I greeted him.

"I'm not Abdul, I'm Mohammad," he said.

At this point, I was for sure convinced that I was being kidnapped.

Mohammad continued, "Abdul is having problems. He couldn't make it. I'm here for you right now."

I was surprised and glad that he spoke English, but at the same time, terrified that this was staged and my money would be stolen, or that my parents would get a phone call asking for one million dollars, or . . . there were a lot of options, all more terrible than the one before.

Turns out that Mohammad was, in fact, a friend and colleague of Abdul's. Abdul finally arrived and apologized for being late. I still didn't know if he was lying about the flat tire, but it didn't matter. I was left with him for the next eight days to explore Yemen.

And those eight days were some of the craziest of my life. We drove more than four hundred miles across a country that very few outsiders have seen in the last decade, visiting lots of small towns and coastal villages, as well as beautiful mountains and valleys. But nothing in Yemen was more impressive to me than Shibam, called "Manhattan of the Desert" for its 500+ towers that were built of mud brick back in the fifteenth century. The town is so iconic that it has been named a UNESCO World Heritage Site, and I will never forget what it was like to see this beauty with my own eyes. Each tower is unique, different colors and sizes, and they are so ancient that it felt like a big gust of wind could collapse them to the ground. I remember how small I felt walking around and looking up, almost like the same feeling I get when wandering around present-day Manhattan. But Shibam is over six hundred years old!

> **It is amazing how old the world is, and though I have seen a lot of destruction across the globe, our history is still standing.**

"So, what do you think of this place?" asked Abdul as I stood there in awe of the towers.

"I'm speechless, man," I admitted. "I can't believe this place exists and nobody that I know has heard of it."

"Yes. It's amazing. But we must move quick because there is danger in this area, and we cannot stay for long. Finish taking your picture and let's go back to the car," warned Abdul, reminding me how much of the world's beauty is hidden by its violence.

We proceeded to drive through al-Qaeda territories—and Abdul was being sketchy the whole time. He kept saying things like, "Don't talk to me about the plan where we're going, because they can tap into my phone or tap into our car. Just go with the flow."

I was thinking, *Oh man, this is brutal.*

But then we started staying in some of the villages along the way, and we began to meet the people, eat, and stay in their homes. I attended a wedding, ate some great street food, and learned about the "khat" culture (a stimulant drug that they chew). I saw many ancient cities and UNESCO World Heritage Sites that blew my mind.

Throughout the trip, Abdul kept asking me questions about my religion. I was a little intimidated, scared to admit that I was Jewish. But finally, one day as we were driving through the country, he shared with me, "I'm Jewish too."

I was shocked as he explained that his family was stuck in the countryside and could not reveal themselves or else they would get executed, just for being Jewish. Abdul has to hide his identity too in public. "My real name is David," he told me.

He pulled a yarmulke out of his pocket, and he told me he keeps Shabbat and the holidays all by himself. Later that week, Abdul and I spent a Friday night lighting the Shabbat candles and eating bread. It was one of the most magical nights of my life.

When I began to say the prayers, he started crying. "That's the same way that we pray."

After eight days, I realized that sometimes the farthest-flung place in the world can bring us back home, returning us to our own cultures, our own families, and our traditions. Even if we risked getting kidnapped by al-Qaeda to get there.

The Three Big Rules for Any Big Adventure

RULE #1—CHANGE YOUR MINDSET

This means believing that you can. Stop listening to all the haters. Stop the doubt. Stop the fear.

My seventh-grade teacher, Ms. O'Daniel, once told me that 90 percent of all thoughts are negative. And she's right. We always think negative thoughts. And so you have to change your mindset to think positive. You have to know that you can do it, and you will do it. If you go into a place somewhere, feeling uneasy or uncertain, then what do you think is going to actually happen when it's time to execute? You're going to fail. Mindset is everything. You have to believe that you can.

RULE #2—TAKE ACTION

My motto in life is JUST GO. I've been wearing those two words across my chest since 2016. And I know, by now, you've heard it enough times too.

JUST GO. Book that flight, call that person, and make that hotel reservation. You have to just do it. The hardest part of anything is to start. In the world of becoming a YouTuber, the hardest thing is to make that first video and press *Upload*. If you want to learn how to code iPhone apps, you have to sign up for that first online class. Want to become a skydiving instructor? Your first jump is waiting for you! You just have to do it. And when you start, everything will somehow fall into place. It always works like that. Trust me!

RULE #3—TRUST YOUR GUT

This is more of an instinctual reaction whenever you arrive some-where, meet someone, or approach something for the first time. Trust your gut.

If your insides tell you that something is suspicious, then don't do it. I always listen to my first instinct. A good example would be taxis. In general, you should ALWAYS take Uber, Lyft, or whatever the local ride sharing app is. The drivers on these apps have their backgrounds checked and go through rounds of interviews and pro-cesses to become drivers. If you do end up taking a taxi, then the chances are much higher of getting kidnapped, robbed, or mugged, as they are a lot less trustworthy.

When I was in Tunisia, all of my things were almost stolen by the taxi driver when he started driving the opposite direction and yelling at me to give him my things. I demanded that he pull over to the side of the freeway, and I jumped out of the car with my bags on my back. Thankfully, another taxi drove by five minutes later and picked me up. Since then, I always use my gut instinct whenever I get in a taxi. If the person feels a little off or sketchy, then I just go to the next one. If you're walking around a street at night and you feel like something isn't right, turn the other way. And obviously, the more you travel, the better you get at judging situations, reading people, and understanding different settings and circumstances.

There are certain cues that people display when they are lying, such as looking off in the distance or tapping their shoes or fingers or breathing heavily, and I've become a master at looking for these things on the road.

The more you learn, the more you learn to trust your gut.

HOW TO STAY SAFE ANYWHERE

Safety is obviously the most important aspect when it comes to any trip. And if you dare to venture into a dangerous country such as Yemen, then I recommend using maps.me. It's an app that allows you to download offline maps so they will work when your phone is on airplane mode or when you don't have a signal. With it, you're able to zoom in and check different cities (and remote areas), and the app will locate everything (hospitals, restaurants, etc.), and a little blue GPS dot will track your live location.

It's very helpful to know where you are heading at any given time, especially in taxis.

Every time I went to my hotel at the end of the night and had a small Wi-Fi signal, I checked in with Deanna and my parents. I also use an app called Life360. It works like the Find My Friends app on the iPhone, where anytime I'm connected to a signal, it'll show where I am to people who are using the app.

Another way to stay safe is by dressing local. In Yemen, for example, if you are a male, it is really important to wear a turban and have a beard, if you can grow one, which I frequently do when I travel. Both are highly respected in Yemeni culture.

And once you are dressed the part, it all comes down to trusting your gut. If you feel like something's not right, you need to act quickly. But don't make a big scene because it's important to stay calm. If there is a problem, you simply cannot freak out. You can't hyperventilate. As I've said earlier, you've just got to stay calm.

At one of the checkpoints in Yemen, I was ordered to get out of my car and searched from head to toe. They made me take off my shirt on the side of the road, and they searched everything on me. I was really tense, but I did remain calm. Had I freaked out, making them think I was guilty, I could have been locked up and put behind bars somewhere—and that is my biggest nightmare.

My biggest stress was that I didn't have a working phone or a SIM card—the SIM cards don't even work unless you are in the big cities. All you can do in those situations is remain calm and focus on your breath.

And have an exit plan.

There was one flight every ten days from a small airport in Seiyun to Cairo, but if I missed the flight, or if it was cancelled, which occurred all the time, then I'd have to drive all the way back to the Oman border, which would have taken at least two days, through a *lot* of dangerous checkpoints.

I was able to make the flight, but I was so scared at the airport security. What if they checked my phone or my camera or my computer and saw all of the footage that I took? What if they thought I was an American spy? I had my drone in my backpack, which is completely forbidden—but they never saw it. I was lucky. I got past security, past immigration, and finally on the flight. I was the only non-Yemeni on board, and I was sweating bullets until the moment that the wheels left the ground.

I made it out safely.

As soon as I got to Cairo, I remember kissing the ground. I was so grateful for the trip that I had just taken to Yemen.

> **Everything in life is a risk, and it's up to you to judge your own risk. It's a risk to walk outside your front door because you could get hit by a car. It's a risk to go skydiving or take a boat ride or play football.**

But ultimately, I have found out that life always has a funny way of working itself out in the end, and now I have some of the craziest stories to tell from Yemen. And it was absolutely worth the risk!

FIND YOUR IRON TRAIN

After the amazing experiences I have had in risky places, I urge you to find your own iron ore train. (Quick disclaimer, this is *not* a recommendation to ride the actual iron train unless you are an experienced traveler and can handle extreme situations.)

There are so many adventures out there that will shape you as a person, push you out of your boundaries, and make you realize how vital it is to feel that adrenaline rush in a foreign place.

When you do something crazy and risky, in the end, you'll have the most amazing memories to look back on for the rest of your life and wild stories to tell your friends and family.

Maybe it's going to Vanuatu in the South Pacific and trying kava with the local tribesmen. Maybe it's overcoming your fear of heights by taking a hot air balloon over beautiful Cappadocia, Turkey. Or perhaps it's rappelling down a waterfall in Paraguay. Maybe it's even trying to learn a language like Portuguese by literally moving to a small town in Brazil and figuring it out on your own. Or going there for a month—you don't have to move there. Maybe it's challenging yourself to make five new local friends when you travel to Burundi in East Africa. Or getting far off the beaten path hitchhiking across New Zealand.

Maybe it's about visiting a place in the next state over and beginning your travels domestically. Maybe it's just going farther from home than you have ever gone before.

No matter what, I urge you to find that adventure. JUST GO! Take that leap of faith. There is no doubt in my mind that you will come out a better person. A stronger person. A more confident person. And that's really the reason why we travel.

You want to be a better version of yourself; you want to be a storyteller, a human who has learned that whether you're riding the iron train or an Amtrak, there is always a big adventure waiting for you.

So, I'll ask you again. What's your iron ore train?

How to Find Adventure

You can use the power of artificial intelligence (ChatGPT) to help recommend a fun adventure. Start with a country that you're interested in—for example, Switzerland. Then go to ChatGPT and type "Give me ten examples of big adventures to take in Switzerland." Or you can even search for epic experiences in your own country (I'm sure there are many that you haven't heard of before). If you aren't a fan of AI, then you can ask your friends or poke around social media. But I'm a big fan of using AI to help make our lives more efficient— and it can come up with some pretty incredible adventures for you, based on your budget, interests, and level of adventure.

There can be a lot of logistical planning involved for an epic journey like the iron ore train in Mauritania or my trip to Yemen, even if a lot of the action is spontaneous. There is a great deal of personal sacrifice that happens (time, money, anxiety)—so it's important to take some time to enjoy the feeling of being complete! Pinch yourself, because these are the memories that you will look back on and remember for the rest of your life. I will never forget the taste of that cup of coffee in Nouadhibou, and it leaves me craving another experience like that. Even as I'm writing this, I am getting goosebumps—and I can't wait to plan my next big adventure!!

In the end, the iron ore train is probably the best travel story that I have to tell my grandkids someday. It was amazing. It was exhilarating. Sometimes, I dream that I'm back on the train, and remember how surreal it was. I plan to take many more iron ore trains in the future, in different forms, in different places, in different cities, with different friends, with more stories to tell. Because that's what life's all about. That's what travel is all about.

It's about remembering that no matter how big the adventure, there is always another one waiting for us, at any moment. And that will never change.

Be Social

Being friendly is all you really need to travel the world (other than a passport). Honestly, you can get a toothbrush and deodorant any-where, but you won't have the same trip if you don't engage with and get to know the people you meet along the road. Opening the door for someone and learning how to say thank you in their language are

PART TWO

📍 Ubangi River, between the Central
African Republic and the Democratic
Republic of the Congo

really, really appreciated. When you're friendly, honest, and transparent, you actually get to be a part of the cultures you visit. You get invited into the culture—to dinner, to tea, to bars, to family celebrations. You get to see how the people in a country actually hang out—not like on a postcard or in a history book—but IRL.

How to Say **"Thank you"** Around the World

Language | Most common way to say hello | *Pronunciation*

Amharic | አመሰግናለሁ Ameseginalehu | *Ameseg-nalehu*

Arabic | شكرًا لك šukran | *Shoe-kran*

Burmese | Kyay Zuu | *Kyay-zoo*

English | Thank you | *Than-kyoo*

Farsi | متشکرم Mam'noon | *Mahm-noon*

Filipino | Salamat | *Sala-mat*

French | Merci | *Mehr-see*

Hebrew | תודה Toda | *Toe-dah*

Indonesian | Terima kasih | *Ter-EE-mah kah-see*

Korean | 감사합니다 Kamsahamnida | *KAM-sah-ham-NEE-da*

Kurdish | Spas | *Spahs*

Pashto | له تاسو مننه Manana | *Mah-nah-nah*

Portuguese | Obrigado | *Oh-bree-gah-doh*

Russian | Спасибо spasiba | *Spuh-SEE-buh*

Samoan | Fa'afetai | *Fahfeti*

Spanish | Gracias | *grah-cee-as*

Swahili | Asante | *Ah-sahn-the*

Turkish | Teşekkürler | *Teh-shek-yoo-lar*

Ukrainian | Дякую Diakuju | *Dya-koo-yoo*

Urdu | شکریہ Shukriya | *Shoo-kree-yah*

📍 Moldova

CHAPTER 5

How to Speak the Language Without Speaking the Language

Whenever people ask me, "What's your favorite country in the world?" I usually tell them Afghanistan.

Afghanistan is near and dear to my heart. I spent five weeks traveling all across seven different provinces alongside my local friend and tour guide, Noor.

That said, many Westerners are scared of Afghanistan because they hear only bad things about it in the news. Since 1979, the country has been in a constant state of war due to its geographical location (right between the Western and Eastern world). Many different countries and religions want to control this precious land, trying to establish a stronger presence in the Middle East to be closer to the natural resources of this incredible region of the world. Unfortunately, the beautiful people of Afghanistan have suffered greatly because of it.

Believe it or not, a lot of tourists and backpackers used to visit Afghanistan—over 170,000 a year in the 1960s. The country was part of the "hippie trail," in which members of the hippie subculture would travel from cities in Europe (often London, Paris, or Copenhagen) through Istanbul and onward to locations in South Asia. Travelers would smoke hash and enjoy the beautiful wonders and culture of Afghanistan. But political changes in the late 1970s (the Soviet invasion of Afghanistan and the revolution in Iran) meant these regions were no longer welcoming to Western travelers.

The first time I went to Afghanistan, in 2018, I got the visa in Kuala Lumpur at the Afghan embassy. I had to literally bribe them to declare that I was going to be safe and okay—it required extra money on the table. I told them I was a YouTuber and I was going to make positive stories about Afghanistan. And they trusted me, so they gave me the visa. And I delivered—my stories there received over fifty million views across multiple platforms and really opened up people's eyes to the lovely people, cuisine, and life of this country.

What I love about Afghanistan is that it is essentially like going back in a time machine to twenty, thirty, forty, even one hundred years ago. Most people still dress in a very traditional style of clothing, a *shalwar kameez*, trousers with a long shirt or tunic. The way that the street vendors make ice cream in the market is still in ice buckets, literally pushing it up and down with their hands. The way they interact also speaks to a different time. They aren't lost in technology or the rat race of the Western world; most people aren't using smartphones. Even in the middle of a twenty-year war, Afghanistan was pure and beautiful, with people negotiating in the markets, strangers inviting you into their homes, and friendships, like the one I made with my guide Noor, lasting forever.

I spent all of my time there before the Taliban took over in 2021, so the reality of Afghanistan today is very different from the one in my memories. Even my dear friend Noor is no longer there, in his country that he loved so much, as he was on the last plane out of Kabul with his wife and two kids. He now lives safely and happily in Melbourne, Australia. Still, when I think of Afghanistan, I think of it as I knew it then: a place where the value in being social, and making human connections even as a traveler, was really confirmed. There are many ways to connect with people, so I want to break this down into different categories.

SMILING IS THE UNIVERSAL LANGUAGE

Afghans speak Dari, which is an offshoot of Farsi. Some ethnic groups also speak Pashto or Hazargi or several others . . . but very few can speak English. And to be honest with you, if you can't speak the language, then it shouldn't be a "make or break" determining factor if you visit a country. I will admit that knowing a few words or phrases in the local language can make your experience a lot more fun and enriching, but it's not necessarily required.

Everybody smiles in the same language. I've always said that smiling is the world's only universal language. I mean, just think about it—how incredible is it that you can communicate with eight billion humans with just a simple smile? And though there might be some nuances, smiling is the easiest way to connect with other people, offering a password of kindness and greeting.

By using body language, you can really communicate anything—if you're hungry, if you're tired, if you need to use the bathroom, you can point and show emotion on your face.

> **Every human on this earth has the same feelings—crying, laughing, loving, screaming. And that really communicates.**

I've been in the jungles of the Central African Republic and communicated with people who have never even seen a white person before. And Afghanistan is no different. Even though it's not really modernized, it doesn't matter. You can always find a way to chat with people just by using body language. Take this as one example: The way that they bake bread in Afghanistan is by attaching the dough to a long stick and then throwing it in a huge circular oven so it sticks on the side. Since bread is also their staple dish, this is the way that you can communicate if you're hungry. If you need to ask someone where a restaurant is, then you can make the motion like you are baking bread, and they will point you in the right direction.

UNDERSTAND THE CULTURE

Before you go to any country, you should do your homework and try to understand the cultural basics. What is their religion? What is their language? What kind of food do they eat? How do they dress themselves? How do they pray?

Why? Because you are a visitor in their country and being respectful is mandatory.

Knowing and appreciating the culture you're visiting before your arrival will quickly earn you friends and guides—but even more than that, you get to really learn about what makes a place and its people special, even before you've set foot on its soil.

You'll need to be on the lookout for certain cues that you may not be used to: gestures such as bowing (in Korea and Japan, it's a proper way to greet someone) or a particular dress code. For instance, most Afghan men cover their heads with a turban. If you want to blend in with the culture, you can get one too. By knowing these things, you'll have a better understanding of your environment.

The fact is that many things are happening around you when you travel that you might not realize if you're not culturally aware. So just by doing a little bit of homework and understanding where you're going—how people dress, how they pray, what they eat—it will go a long way in understanding the culture so you can speak to people without knowing the language!

KNOW THE RELIGION

In many countries and cultures, it's extremely important for tourists to be aware of the region's dominant religion.

Afghanistan is a very conservative, strict Islamic country. And within Islam, there are specific laws and rules and regulations that everyone must follow. In regard to women, they do not like to be photographed in public nor have any physical contact with any male who is not their husband—these are not laws, but they are customs, which everyone should respect. Also, women usually are not seen driving cars. We can make our own arguments about how we feel about these rules, but by knowing these things about Islam, you're already prepared for what to expect and how to communicate with people.

Friday night prayer is a really important time for Muslims. By knowing that, you can be more sensitive around that time of the evening on Friday. If it's Ramadan, you must know that they're fasting from sunrise to sunset, so do not bring your own food to eat in public places—in Afghanistan, it's actually illegal to do that. (And don't even think about drinking alcohol in countries like Iran, Egypt, or Saudi Arabia, or you will be thrown in jail! See "The Basic Rules of Partying" just up ahead.)

All of these things are vital to know so you can have a safe experience in the country while respecting and understanding the culture.

The Basic Rules of Partying

People all over the world love to party and drink and enjoy the company of others. Even if they choose not to drink, they still go out and have fun! And that's what it's all about. If you smoke and/or drink and are planning to do so while you're traveling, you have to know what the smoking and drinking rules are in each country. There may be limitations you don't anticipate.

Smoking: Pretty much the whole world, even strict Muslim countries, smokes cigarettes. The USA (and other Western nations) are the only places I've seen where tobacco is considered "taboo." Do keep in mind that some countries have bans on smoking in public, so if you're not sure, Google the rules before you go. Smoking can be a great conversation starter, depending on the country you are in. If you don't smoke cigarettes, buy somebody a beer at the bar or simply give them a dollar in your home currency (I've found this to be a fantastic gift and everyone appreciates it as a souvenir). These little things go a long way.

When it comes to weed, it's only fully legal in some US states, Canada, Georgia (the country), Malta, Mexico, South Africa, Thailand, Jamaica, and Uruguay. It's decriminalized in a few other nations (notably the Netherlands), and it is *very illegal* in most of the world.

Drinking: There are a handful of "dry countries," which means that it's forbidden and illegal to sell, purchase, or consume alcohol within them. You can go to jail for drinking alcohol. The countries are Libya, Kuwait, Afghanistan, Mauritania, Saudi Arabia, Somalia, Iran, Sudan, and Yemen.

All of the nations where alcohol is forbidden are majority Muslim; liquor is banned in the Quran, and many Muslim countries tend to take a dim view of drinking. That said, for a "dry" country, Sudan is where I went to one of the wildest parties of my life! I ended up going to the British embassy of all places, because while alcohol is forbidden in Sudan, it's allowed at embassies. (Let's just say that the Brits know how to throw a party. There was a full-on bouncer at the door, you had to pay a cover fee to get in—and there was music, and drinks were flowing left and right. All UK embassies in the world follow UK laws.) I met a lot of cool people that night, not only Brits, but mostly Sudanese. It was one of those moments where I had to pinch myself and ask, "Am I in Sudan or New York right now?" It was the most unexpected night of my life.

In other Muslim countries such as Egypt, Morocco, and Syria, it's legal to consume alcohol only in certain places (like hotel bars, for example). The hotel nightclubs in Doha, Qatar (another dry country), rival that of Las Vegas, and you can dance the night away until 5 AM.

Aside from Muslim-majority countries, most of the rest of the world drinks alcohol.

Drugs: It's safe to say that unless the country is called the Netherlands, then all hardcore drugs are illegal (and even in the Netherlands, there are some gray legal areas, so be careful!). Basically, I do NOT recommend trying them unless you want to sit behind bars.

SHARE MUSIC AND LEARN HOW TO DANCE

Along with food (which we'll get to in a minute) and historical sites, music is one of the best parts about traveling the world. Every country and culture has its own music. Italy has a vibrant opera scene. In Papua New Guinea, they have distinctive wooden instruments. In Sweden, they're notoriously skilled at playing the piano and singing. It's really helpful to know these things so you can understand and appreciate the culture.

In Afghanistan, there is a traditional wooden instrument called a rubab. I first heard it in the central, mountainous region called Bamiyan, where a twenty-something-year-old girl played it for me inside of her living room, and the sound was magical. (Afghanistan bans women from playing any musical instruments in public spaces.)

A great travel tip is to learn about the traditional music, artists, and songs before you enter the country, so it's a common point of conversation. Maybe have some photos or videos of your own famous local musicians on your phone to share with other musicians. That will get you some new friends who are excited to share their culture with you!

In Afghanistan and Iran, people dance by waving their arms and hands in slow circular movements up in the air. People love to dance and sing and listen to music—that's why there is such a huge wedding culture! Afghans really are the most welcoming and humble people on our planet, and they have gone through hell and back by surviving the last fifty-five years in a constant state of civil war.

BE OPEN

It seems like, for many Americans, it is getting tougher and tougher to be open to spontaneous social interactions with strangers. We can be closed off or absorbed in our smartphones. But especially when you're traveling, being open to conversation can take you places you don't expect—literally.

When I was in Bangui, Central African Republic, my local friend David introduced me to another local tour guide, a guy named Edgar, who took me on a seven-hour journey deep into the jungle to meet the Pygmy tribe. The Pygmies are genetically the shortest people in the world and only live in the jungles of Central Africa (Gabon, Cameroon, and Central African Republic). I got to sleep overnight in their huts, dance by the campfire, and was able to make a ten-minute documentary on their fascinating lifestyle. It was an experience I'll never forget.

When I was in Tunisia, I met two brothers on the street in the old Medina (city center). I told them I was a tourist and I really wanted to learn about their country. In response, they invited me over to their house. Their mom cooked me the most amazing Tunisian food, and we had a great evening together, chatting by the fire and talking about life. The brothers told me about their hometown in the southern part of the Tunisian desert. They educated me about all the wars and conflicts that have happened in Tunisia, such as the birth of the Arab Spring in 2011—a political uprising by the young generation in response to the corruption and slow economic growth of the country. The Arab Spring later spread to Egypt and across North Africa and the Middle East, leading to street demonstrations of millions of people chanting, "The people want to bring down the regime."

The brothers gave me an excellent perspective and understanding about Tunisian life. They even demanded that I sleep in their room while they slept on the floor.

For that night, I wasn't just visiting a country, I was a part of a family.

And guess what? We can all be a part of it if we're willing to be friendly.

EAT THE FOOD

Fact: Food is the ultimate connector. There's no quicker way to bond with someone than over a meal. Why? Because everybody needs to eat. It's that simple. Having conversations around the dinner table is universal, in every culture in the world. Breaking bread means the same thing everywhere even if you're not actually eating bread. People get to know each other as they eat; it connects us in ways that few other activities can. And much like music, each country (and often even each region within that country) will offer you amazing, different dishes to try. From Mexican tacos to Japanese sushi to Nigerian fufu to Yemeni goat to Indian curry—it's best to embrace all foods from around the world.

In Afghanistan, people still drink tea and prepare the food while sitting on the floor. When I first arrived in Kabul and met my tour guide, Noor, he took me to a local spot where it was customary to remove your shoes and sit directly on the floor. The waiter brings thin plastic mats that you put over the floor for sanitary reasons and then starts serving tea and food. I remember thinking how special this experience was, and I was impressed that Afghanistan still holds on to much of its tradition in today's world.

The best meal of my life happened in Karbala, Iraq (more on that trip in the next chapter). A friend of a friend of my local tour guide, Baderkhan, found out that we were in Karbala, and he invited us into his house for dinner at the last minute. He was stressed because he said that he had no time to prepare the meal, but in fact, it was one of the *biggest meals* that you can imagine. We all sat on the floor in the traditional style and were served plate after plate of meat (lamb, goat, chicken) and rice, and then fresh fruit, yogurt, almonds, and cashews. It was just a random Thursday afternoon, and the way that they prepared the meal and hosted us really shows a lot about their kindness.

The family that I met asked me about America. The man's wife told me, "You know, people here in Iraq idolize America. We love your culture, your movies, and, especially, your music. We try to look past the wars and the politics and connect with the people. We are honored to meet you and host you in our house." I had the chance to show them who we were from the inside—to show them that Americans are kind and generous people who help our neighbors and believe in freedom and hope.

While I was working on this book, I traveled to Tokyo. It was so nice to be back in Japan after the country was closed to travelers for two and a half years during the pandemic! I love Tokyo—it's one of the greatest cities in the world. My favorite part of my trip was discovering this little tucked-away neighborhood called Omoide Yokocho. It's a bunch of winding streets that are filled with tiny, and I mean TINY, bars and restaurants that fit no more than five people in each place. You just walk in, greet the bartender/chef, and sit down while they serve you whatever they are cooking or preparing that night. It's so amazing!

While the Tokyo Tower and various shrines around the city are worthwhile to visit, the lasting memories are the other experiences, like the little bars, the conversations, and meals you will never forget. They include the incredible meal from a street food vendor and the dinner at a stranger's home where language isn't even needed. I encourage you to go into local restaurants and try local dishes with local people. Try street food or offer someone a free meal. A simple act of kindness goes a long way. And it's one of the best ways (if not the best) to make new friends as well.

Food is, and always will be, one of the best parts of traveling. Not to mention, it's a great way to speak to someone without knowing the language!

Cross-Cultural Influences

One of the coolest things you'll experience as you travel is getting to understand how different world cultures have influenced one another. For instance, Windhoek, Namibia, has great nightlife for a reason I didn't anticipate. Did you know that the country was colonized by Germany? That means that they brought their beer over, and there are so many breweries today that serve some of the tastiest beer in the entire world. One brewery was open 24-7, and on a Tuesday night, I went out and made some Namibian friends that I still talk to to this day!

Now, sometimes you will still be pushed out of your comfort zone in different ways. I was traveling in Siberia, the far east of Russia, inside of a city called Yakutsk. It's actually considered one of the world's coldest cities (I get cold just thinking about it). It was –40°C when I was there. Side note, Celsius and Fahrenheit meet at minus forty.

When I went inside a coffee shop, I approached a guy sitting at a table and asked him what was going on with a very simple gesture. In this instance, though I didn't speak the language, I got lucky (which sometimes happens!). He told me, "Oh, I speak English. Nice to meet you. My name is Chris."

It turned out that his family lived in a little fishing village about forty-five minutes outside the city. So, they took me in the car, invited me inside their house, and I sat down with them at their kitchen table for dinner. They served fresh sashimi and raw horse meat (a local delicacy—and trust me, the friendlier you are, the more you will also be invited to sample local delicacies, for better or worse). They told me everything about their land and how much it means to have livestock and cattle. Chris's mother was a shaman. She was a deeply spiritual woman with a strong connection with nature. She talked to the trees, to her animals, and she explained how humans had historically been able to survive in this cold tundra. I was also introduced to their cousins, who lived next door. By the end of the day, I had made friends with the entire village through this amazing family.

Because every village is open to us, every local delicacy is there for you to try (or not to try). You can quite literally visit anywhere (if it's at the right time), and as long as you are friendly, you will experience the world in ways you didn't know were possible.

> **You will have so many moments that feel like they are out of a different time or a different life, sitting among the locals, and realizing just how alike we truly are (minus the raw horse meat bit).**

Sometimes it's okay to be pushed outside your comfort zone. In a situation like this, if you are ever offered a food that you aren't ready for or aren't comfortable eating, the best thing you can do is smile, embrace it, and give it a try. The worst thing that can happen is you don't like the taste, or it makes you gag, but more often than not, the only consequence is that you get respect from the people around you.

And look, sometimes, you can make fun of yourself and offer a reason you can't eat it, but as much as you are able to try, the more you'll connect with other cultures—and their foods.

I have plenty of friends in my phone book who don't speak a word of English. But in the modern age, all we need is Google Translate to text each other. Just like my friend Hussain, who I met at a pomegranate stand in Syria. I was showing him pictures on my phone of my travels on the side of the street in Damascus, and it was a special moment. Or that time in

Hanoi, Vietnam, when I got a haircut on the street. I became friends with my barber, Trong, and we still are in touch to this day.

All these situations have come up because I understood the culture at a beginner's level, as well as having some courage. And a smile goes a really long way when you can't speak a language.

Even today, the moment you put down this book, go walk outside and smile at someone. I guarantee you that they'll smile back unless they're having a terrible day. Especially in other countries, when they know you're a tourist, you have an advantage because they will appreciate that you're visiting their country.

The good news is you can start practicing your travel skills at home right now. You can go to the restaurant off the beaten track, you can invite a stranger to dinner, or you can open your own home to a visitor in your town (and if you have a refugee population, you can extend the same invite that has often been extended to me in their home countries).

You can start to get out of your comfort zone while in your comfort zone, and you can begin to see the world from your own front yard.

But hopefully, that just won't be enough for you. You will begin to crave the street food in Bangkok, you will want to hear Arab music in the Middle East, and you will no longer be content to stay. You will need to JUST GO.

I hope this chapter has given you a little bit more courage to realize that there are many people out there who don't know you yet but would love to be your friend. As the saying goes, "A stranger is a friend you haven't met yet." And believe me, they're out there.

📍 Modadishu, Somalia

CHAPTER 6

Make New Friends (The Internet Helps)

My golden rule for travel is to make a local friend (or friends)—no matter where you go in the world. You will hear me repeat this a lot throughout this book. If I didn't make local friends, then I would have struggled to visit every country and therefore wouldn't be writing this book, plain and simple. Local friends are tremendously helpful for navigation, translation, and safety. And frankly, it's nice to get to learn about a country through the eyes of someone who is from there.

And don't feel like you're "imposing" on your contacts, because there's truth in the saying "what goes around, comes around." If a friend of a friend visited you in your hometown, you would be more than happy to take them around, wouldn't you? When you think about it, meeting and spending time with locals is a win-win. Having a local friend is a cultural exchange for both parties. They show you their culture and, in return, they get to learn about yours. I've had a lot of friends come and visit me in the States too, so I have been able to return the favor. There's nothing like hanging out with a buddy you met in Oman two years later in downtown Los Angeles.

> **Making connections can be a surreal experience—and they're part of what makes travel worth the money, the stress, the long nights in airports, and even longer days.**

But you've got to make sure that you make *friends*, not just "contacts" or "acquaintances." I'm talking about people who you can rely on, and people who you can trust—and I'll admit that it's sometimes hard to find these people. That leads us to Bashar—my local friend in Juba, South Sudan.

FIND YOUR BASHAR

As you might know, South Sudan is one of the most dangerous countries in the world. The nation was in a twenty-two-year civil war with its northern counterpart (Sudan) mainly due to different religions and beliefs—the north being Muslim and the south being Christian. In 2011, South Sudan broke off as the newest UN-recognized country in the world, and since then, political instability, turmoil, and economical disasters have taken over, leading it to be the poorest country in Africa and not a place to visit alone.

Thankfully, a few days before my trip, I was able to get in touch with thirty-two-year-old Bashar through Instagram. I posted on my IG Stories: "Hey guys, I'm heading to South Sudan in a few days and looking for local friends to show me around, please DM me if you know anyone!" And twenty-four hours later, I received a DM from Bashar.

Standing at six feet five with short black hair and glasses, Bashar is originally from Somalia, but he became a refugee and walked across the border into Kenya at a young age. Nowadays, he's a self-made multimillionaire and entrepreneur—who never went to a day of school in his life. He lives in Juba, South Sudan's capital, and runs his business from there. Bashar has been able to create an entire supplies company from the ground up, importing things from mosquito nets to chairs from around the world. He works closely with the UN and other humanitarian aid services, and his office is amazing. He kindly offered to take me around Juba and show me what's going on. If it wasn't for him, I would have had a very tough time navigating the streets and using my camera. Filming is illegal unless you have permission, but he was able to get me a camera permit to shoot anywhere. Throughout my time in Juba, Bashar wouldn't let me pay for anything. I don't always appreciate that, because I always like to give my part, but he insisted on paying, and it was really nice of him.

And I must say that I had a great time in Juba, while most of my other friends struggled there. But Bashar showed me the country like a local, taking me to his favorite restaurants where we ate goat, which had been slow cooked in the ground, just as people have been doing for centuries.

We cruised down the Nile River (yes, it goes all the way down to Juba!), smoking shisha (or a hookah, which is a tobacco water pipe that is famous in the Middle East and North Africa) to cap off our great days. To this day, the second most viral video I've ever posted on my YouTube is called "The World's Tallest Humans"—which I made in South Sudan with Bashar.

The thing is, we can all find our own Bashar.

The beauty of travel doesn't come from making acquaintances but building real friendships, ones we keep with us for a long time after we have gone, and making it more likely that we will return.

I understand it might be a little daunting at first to blindly go into a place and meet someone for the first time in person (especially someone that you met on social media), but, as I've said, 99 percent of people in this world are good people. They're not out to hurt you. They're there to help you. And they are genuinely curious to learn more about your life, in the same way that you're curious to know more about them and their culture.

Six Steps to Making Your Own New Friends

The following are the best methods and practices that I use to create local connections.

1. Ask your friends—At least a month prior to your trip, find a friend who you know has been to a particular country and ask them for any contacts! Then simply message or call that contact and let them know your situation. If you aren't sure if any of your friends have traveled to a particular place, you can broaden your outreach on social media (see #3).

2. Search hashtags—Use Instagram and look up common hashtags related to travel in that country. If you were planning a trip to Vietnam, for instance, you could search hashtags like #vietnamtravel, #visitvietnam, #travelingtovietnam, #hanoi, #saigon, etc. Spend some time scrolling and looking at the posts, see who is posting currently in Vietnam, and then DM them! It sounds creepy, but isn't that what social media is in a nutshell—creeping on other people's lives? I'm kidding, but really, social media is about making connections. By this point, so many of us have made IRL friendships from the internet, and travel buddies are no different.

3. Search or post on social media—On Facebook, search for groups using keywords such as "[Name of Country] Travel," and then join them (or request to join if they're private). You post a message in there and tell people your travel plans and see if anyone there is willing to meet you. Alternatively, you could post on IG Stories or X (formerly Twitter) and open up the question to people in your network.

📍 **Kabushiya, Sudan** | Approaching the Pyramids of Meroë, a UNESCO World Heritage Site that doesn't get much tourism. The burial sites around the ancient city of Meroë date back to the third century BCE.

📍 **Bogotá, Colombia** | This was my first country in South America and my first day exploring it! Bogotá was everything I dreamed it would be—friendly people, tasty coffee, and amazing architecture— and to this day, it remains as one of my favorite cities.

📍 **Samarra, Iraq** | Standing with a soldier in front of the spiral minaret of the Great Mosque of Samarra.

📍 **Queenstown, New Zealand** | Flying above stunning fjords and mountains Down Under!

📍 **One hour outside Beijing, China** | Witnessing beauty on the Great Wall. Fun fact: it would take you more than 17 months to walk the full length of the Great Wall. Most often, visitors choose to spend just a day or two seeing a section of this incredible structure.

📍 **Dibab, Oman** | The Bimmah Sinkhole, with ocean views behind. This turquoise blue lake sits in a sinkhole that is more than 300 feet deep in the deepest part. And it's located less than half a mile from the sea!

📍 **Herat, Afghanistan** | In front of the Friday Mosque, which is considered Afghanistan's finest Islamic building. It is covered in bright mosaic tile!

📍 **Wahiba Sands, Oman** | Camping overnight with nomads in the heart of eastern Oman.

📍 **Cairo, Egypt** | Filming at the Pyramids of Giza.

South Sudan | With one of the Mundari tribe, a small ethnic group in South Sudan. The Mundari people's economy centers on livestock, particularly their famous cattle known for their huge horns! South Sudan gained independence from the Republic of Sudan in 2011, making it the world's youngest country (as of this writing).

Somewhere in the countryside of Turkmenistan | Drinking tea, especially green tea, is a huge part of Turkmen culture (tea culture is strong in the rest of Asia, too).

Kathmandu, Nepal | Hanging with my new friends in Kathmandu, the capital of Nepal.

Chinatown, Singapore | Taking a break for some noodles with a friend in my favorite hawker center (open-air food court) in Chinatown.

◉ Karbala, Iraq | Standing where one of the biggest Shi'ite pilgrimages occurs each year. The city's population is estimated at 711,000 or so, but more than 10 million Shi'ite Muslims visit annually.

◉ Varanasi, Uttar Pradesh, India | Getting marked in Varanasi, which is a holy city in the Hindu faith that draws many pilgrims every year.

📍 **Duhok, Iraq** | Iraqi Kurdistan is an autonomous region in the northern part of Iraq. There, they have their own flag, currency, and government, but it's still technically part of Iraq, by the UN's standards.

📍 **Rio de Janeiro, Brazil** | Selfie with Christ the Redeemer, one of the "New 7 Wonders of the World." (The other six are the Great Wall of China, Colosseum, Taj Mahal, Chichen Itza, Petra, anwd Macchu Picchu.)

📍 **Cappadocia, Turkey** | The Cappadocia region of central Turkey is famous for its cone-shaped rock formations sometimes called "fairy chimneys." The best way to see them? By hot air balloon!

4. Couchsurfing.com and MeetUp.com—Both of these websites are so useful! Simply create a free profile, tell people where you are going, and start looking for local friends who have the same interests as you.

5. ToursByLocals.com—I've used this website three or four times, and it's always been great. Get connected with local guides who will take you around their city. It costs some money—I think I paid $150 for my last tour in Okinawa—but it was well worth it!

6. Meet people in person! This is one strategy you obviously can't use in advance. Walk into a bar, a café, or a souvenir shop and talk to people. It takes a little bit of courage, but believe me when I say that "life begins at the end of your comfort zone!" Try your hotel concierge or Airbnb host—tell them that you are looking for a local person to walk around town with you. Nine times out of ten, it'll work. That's how I got in touch with Anton, in Luanda, Angola! We are still friends to this day.

Also, if you have any special interests, that's a great way to meet people. If you play soccer, you can join a local football match or find the football community of the town you are in. If you're part of a local cultural organization or club—anything from knitting to EDM music to recovery programs—there are probably international analogs, so check out meetups online and meet the locals. There is no shortage of like-minded people around the world who are just like you in so many ways; they just happen to come from another country!

BECOME YOUR OWN DREW BINSKY—AND
SHARE THE WORLD WITH OTHERS

By being friendly, you don't just get to be a part of the world. You also get to share it with other people, in turn.

When I was in La Paz, Bolivia, I met a man named Rodrigo because I was friendly to him in a local market. We started chatting, and when he found out that I was a tourist, he invited me to visit the famous Uyuni Salt Flats—the largest body of salt in the world. He drove me and my now wife Deanna seven hours in his truck. Now, here's the thing: I was filming along the journey, and I was able to come back and share that experience with my viewers.

We all have our own ways to share the world with others. What's yours? Before we continue, I want you to think about that. How can you share the world with other people? Through social media? Through pictures? Through writing? Maybe it's just a matter of sending ten postcards from every place you visit—or sharing your videos with ten million viewers on YouTube. I promise you both ways will help others change how they see the world. (In fact, I'll share some of the secrets to my YouTube success in chapter thirteen.)

> **When we share our adventures, we not only connect with people who are also out there traveling, we inspire people who aren't traveling to consider that it's possible—and worth every dime, time, and challenge!**

The bottom line is that you have to make local friends—it's the only way to really maximize your experience in a limited time. And I must say that after traveling nonstop for more than eleven years, I have built up quite the database of contacts in different countries. In fact, you can type any country in the search bar on my phone, and someone will come up (tip: always save people's names as FIRST NAME and then COUNTRY [FROM]—it's helpful later on!).

If you are paranoid about meeting "strangers," then I recommend Face-Timing them in advance. Research their social media and use your best judgment and your gut instinct before you meet them. Also, I'm aware that traveling as a white male can make meeting people easier—although traveling as a Jew in the Arab world definitely has its risks as well. But always do what feels right and safest for you. If that means only meeting up with people of your gender, or through verified touring agencies, that's fine too.

And then from there on, you JUST GO have fun.

TRAVELING LIKE A LOCAL TAKES KNOWING ONE

Let's stay on the topic of Sudan—but now, we're heading to the northern part. It's very different from South Sudan, which is why they split into two countries. They have different religions, different languages, different cultural traditions, and totally different vibes on the streets.

My local friend in Sudan was named Mazin. He's a fellow content creator, and we connected over our mutual love of YouTube.

What a journey we had together! He picked me up when I arrived in Khartoum, the bustling capital city, and then we went on a crazy road trip. Did you know that Sudan has more pyramids than Egypt? The Nubian pyramids are located at various sites along the Nile. The most extensive site is near the ancient city of Meroë. It's located in the historical homelands of the Nubian tribe, which is full of beautiful people who are living in villages of circular-shaped white houses. Some of them have pet crocodiles, which is kind of terrifying but also, really cool.

The pyramids at Meroë are not built for tourism. There are no pretty souvenir shops or bathrooms or buildings with air-conditioning. As soon as we rolled up, there was a little guy on a camel who greeted us and opened the makeshift rope gate.

"Welcome to the ancient kingdom of Meroë," he murmured.

We paid a small fee of five dollars USD and then we had the whole place to ourselves! It was amazing. I was even able to fly my drone (because no officials were around us), which is usually a no-no on most of the African continent—especially UNESCO World Heritage Sites like this one. I'll never forget watching the sunset over the beautiful desert and peeking right through the cracks of the pyramids. Also, being able to walk freely across the pyramids and see the hieroglyphics and learn about them was truly amazing!

Mazin guided me into the dark room inside one of the pyramids with only a beam of sunlight shining on the writings on the stone and said to me while pointing his finger, "Drew, do you see this? It is written in the ancient Meroitic script, which became extinct almost two thousand years ago. Can you imagine what life was like back then?"

"This is one of the coolest things I've ever seen, man," I said as I shook my head in wonder. "And the craziest thing is that nobody knows about it!"

And Sudan just kept getting better. I mean, as soon as we returned to the city, we stopped by these older ladies on the side of the road who were making and serving piping hot tea in the hot weather. Sudan is one of the hottest places I've ever been—think 115°F or 46°C. This tea culture comes from the Arabic influence, which is interesting because (north) Sudan has a mix of Arab settlers, whereas its southern counterpart is much more indigenous. In Sudan, they have browner skin and speak more of a proper Arabic dialect, and in South Sudan, they have very dark skin and speak what they call "Juba Arabic."

ONE LAST ADVENTURE WITH BASHAR

Bashar has been super helpful for me, not only in Juba, but in Somalia, too. He also was my guide in Mogadishu—the capital city. Although he didn't grow up there, his first language is Somali, and he has a lot of contacts there.

When asked, "What is the most dangerous city in the world?" my answer based on my own personal travel experience is Mogadishu. I've never been more scared of getting kidnapped or mugged in any other city in the world (and that doesn't mean I didn't still love it or appreciate its people). But since 1991 (my birth year), Somalia has been in a constant state of civil war with many kidnappings, armed attacks, robberies, and frequent explosions. In fact, the Hyatt across the street from my hotel in Mogadishu was completely blown up a couple months after I left. So was the ice cream shop next door where I enjoyed a cone. The reason for all of this turmoil is an al-Qaeda–linked terrorist group called al-Shabaab, which is trying to establish a presence and control the Somali government. This issue, combined with the devastating humanitarian crisis in which half of the city's population is facing acute food insecurity and malnutrition, is the reason why you will see a huge UN presence (with their big white trucks and the word *UN* written in big black letters on the sides).

I am always conscious of the fact that I may not be able to make a return trip to certain places I loved. Some places have disappeared altogether in the years, months, or mere weeks since I was able to visit—a market in Iraq, the hotel in Mogadishu, and in many ways, the Afghanistan I used to know. Although there are a million different places off the beaten path where you can travel, there are also many places that in their current political climates would not be safe for most travelers to go.

Mogadishu is one of those places.

Of course, I was with Bashar the whole time, but it was still intense! We got picked up from the airport in a bulletproof pickup truck with blacked-out windows, with four armed bodyguards sitting on the truck bed. To get to our hotel, we drove a mile through a maze fortress with big ten-foot-tall sandbags and checkpoints with officers who had AK-47s strapped to their chests. We finally got to our hotel, and—after the security check that was more intense than any airport—we were greeted by the hotel owner (coincidentally also named Bashar) and then brought downstairs, below the lobby, into the basement for a briefing. This was straight out of a movie!

There were fifteen big TV screens and all these controls. And he sat us down, pulled up a live map of the city, and explained that he had planted surveillance cameras all over the city to look around 24-7. He pulled up Google Maps, and there were hundreds of red flags on the map of Mogadishu. Each flag, he explained, was either a terrorist attack, a bombing, or a kidnapping within the last twelve months.

He proceeded to tell us the do's and don'ts—be careful, don't leave the hotel without guards, be under constant supervision, don't speak to police, etc. It was absolutely crazy. Every time we left the hotel, we were in an armored vehicle, with a car in front and a car in back, each with four armed military guards with helmets on and bulletproof chest protection and large guns.

When we'd arrive to a location—say a lighthouse on the beach—the group of armed guards would have to scout it out, jumping over fences to look through cracks. And then, we'd have ten to fifteen minutes to wander around the different sites before getting back into the car and moving on.

You might wonder, why go to such great lengths? Why put myself in such danger?

Because we can't fully understand the world until we're willing to see all of it, even the hardest parts.

Mogadishu was actually a beautiful, tropical place at one point, and though it's tragic what has happened between the warring factions that fight over it, it was amazing to meet the people and be reminded that even in the worst of circumstances, humans still just want to be known and just want to be human. Not to mention, that beach is a serious candidate for the most beautiful in Africa. For Bashar, the trip held its own meaning. It was the first time that he had established a strong emotional connection with Mogadishu. Being a Somali refugee, he never had the chance to experience Mogadishu in his adult life, but yet, he remains so connected with his culture and the lifestyle. It was also the first time that he was able to show a friend around Somalia, and because of this, I think we both felt incredibly honored.

And I never could have done it without Bashar. As we stood on the beach, looking out at the crystal-blue sea, so peaceful and calming, he shared with me, "My bro, we did it. No tourist ever comes to Mogadishu. But you were bold enough to come and see the *real* culture and get the *real* stories. Thank you, my friend. We will never forget this trip."

The stories from Mogadishu and Juba ended up garnering more than forty million views on social media. But it wasn't about racking up numbers, it was about showing the world the other sides of these countries that we might have heard about in the news, or watched a story about in the movies, but that most will likely never see with their own eyes. (Again, I don't recommend anyone visit these places alone, without a local friend, unless you really are adventurous and will assume all risks. In the meantime, you have my YouTube for some of the wilder adventures.) Going there was a chance to meet the people of Somalia and Sudan, to understand that war is rarely waged by the people on the ground. Most of the people I have met on my travels have only wanted peace—they want to go to school and to go to work; they want to fall in love and start families; they want to go out and dance.

Bashar is more than just a networking buddy or guide; he's become a true friend. Because when you're out there traveling with someone, learning about their culture, sharing your own, your relationship evolves quickly. If you've connected with the right person, you are building a true and lasting friendship. When I left, Bashar said, "You always have a home in East Africa, and I will be waiting for your next visit."

Friendships are everything to me. Not only to help me travel to faraway places, but to meet those friends again in the future! I talk to Bashar and Mazin on a monthly basis. Both of them have invited me back to Africa, to spend some time in Somalia, Sudan, and South Sudan. I'm really grateful for the friendships I have with them and all my other local friends around the world.

Now, after years of travel, I can just open up my WhatsApp, and within two seconds, I can message someone on the other side of the globe. Of course, if they ever came to the US, or wherever I'm living at the time, I'm more than happy to show them around and be their guide. Because that's when it comes full circle. The world can be a really cool place, and that's the beauty of travel—we realize how similar and connected and cool we all really are.

📍 Al Shaheed Monument, Baghdad, Iraq

CHAPTER 7

Look Past the Outsides

For nearly as long as I have been alive, there has been a war in Iraq in which the United States has been involved. If someone told you they were going to Iraq, you'd assume it was as a member of the armed forces—never as a tourist. There's a reason for that; the country was essentially off-limits to American tourists for a long while, until they opened up the visa policy in 2019. That's when I decided to go on a two-week trip with my Spanish friend, Alvaro, who has also been to every country.

My local friend, Baderkhan, flew to meet Alvaro and me at the airport in Baghdad. I'd met Baderkhan a few years earlier in Iraqi Kurdistan, an autonomous region in the northern part of Iraq. Baderkhan was born in Baghdad, but he's Kurdish and he still lives in Kurdistan—which is *very* different than Iraq proper. There, they have their own flag, currency, and government, but it's still technically part of Iraq, by the UN's standards.

For the next two weeks, we road-tripped around the country—and when I say it was crazy, I mean it was *crazy*. We went from Baghdad to Samarra—which has one of the tallest and oldest minarets on Earth. Then we went to Karbala, where the world's biggest pilgrimage takes place to honor a Shiite prophet. After that we moved to Babylon, the birthplace of humanity and the very first civilization. And finally, we took a tour through the Mesopotamian marshlands in a place called Chibayish—a UNESCO site where you can only get around by boat.

Being with Baderkhan made everything so much easier! He's a hilarious guy and a traveler himself—he has visited seventy countries—so he is a great guide for navigating the cultural differences between his country and the West, but he's also very Iraqi.

During that trip, I discovered that Iraq is the gem of the Middle East. There is so much beauty in Iraqi culture that nobody hears about on the news. There's also so much rich history there, in the place where East meets West. The cradle of civilization—the land of ancient Mesopotamia—between the Tigris and Euphrates rivers. Home of the world's first city, Babylon, dating back to 2300 BCE. Babylon is so cool. The famous blue gate with hieroglyphics of animals and ancient inscriptions greets you, and then you walk deeper into the settlement that once was the largest city in the world. But when I was there, we had the entire site pretty much to ourselves (one upside of traveling in a country with little tourism).

We headed to Karbala, where the Arba'een Pilgrimage—the world's largest annual gathering—takes place every October. More than twenty million Shiite Muslims march to the center of Karbala, where Imam Hussain's tomb is, to pay respect to their leaders. It's such a spiritual place, and it was such a treat to be able to go there and document and tell stories.

Then of course you have Baghdad, the capital city, which is filled with color and beauty and markets and all kinds of street food.

Iraq is one of those places that is always on your mind once you leave. You might leave Iraq, but truly, it will never leave you.

As I was going on my last trip, I thought back to all the things I had heard about Iraq, imagining a country of terrorism and suicide bombers, violence and anger. But my trip was filled with beautiful people just trying to rebuild their lives. Once again, I was reminded that travel is the ultimate stereotype buster, showing us that the things we have learned or thought or assumed about a group of people are usually based on one element or aspect of the place, but they very rarely apply to all.

Because travel teaches us to not judge people by their politicians or whatever we hear in the news cycle; it shows us who we really are—all humans, steeped in history, trying to survive in whatever ways we know how. Travel helps you see past myths about cultures. When we grow up in our little bubbles—whether it's an American bubble or Brazilian bubble or Japanese bubble—everything that we learn about in our public (and private) school classrooms is biased. The only way to get an unbiased judgment of any place is to physically go there yourself. Look people in the eyes, sit down with them at dinner, and listen to them. That's the only way you will truly understand a place, in my opinion. It teaches you to have empathy, so you can put yourself in other people's shoes and feel their emotional state. It's so important. This is why travel makes us better people.

FIND THE SIMILARITIES

Misunderstandings about certain cultures' religious beliefs are some of the most persistent stereotypes around. And wars fought over religion have caused millions and millions of deaths around the world. So when we talk about looking past the outsides, we have to talk about religion.

I grew up Jewish, went to Hebrew school, had a bar mitzvah. I am still a proud Jew and honored to be a part of a religion that makes up 0.2 percent of the world's population, but I've become more agnostic, and more open, as I've traveled the world. What I've realized is that all religions teach essentially the same things about what it means to be a good person: Don't lie, don't cheat, don't steal, give to the poor, and look out for your community. I've been in thousands of mosques around the world, including dozens around Iraq, and I love how peaceful they are. I love the values of Muslim people and the oneness of humanity.

Religion should not separate us; it should bind us. Beyond our shared ethical principles (which are also core tenets of Christianity), Jews and Muslims are *so* similar. We both pray to one god, we both fast on various days of the year, we have similar diets (kosher and halal), and we both even wear small hats on our heads! But the similarities don't end there—we both love eating, we both give back to the poor, we both have a special prayer on Friday nights. Hebrew and Arabic are similar and are both read from right to left. If that doesn't show that we are brothers, then I don't know what does!

Another religion with similar core principles is Sikhism, which is practiced throughout the world but is especially prominent in India. Despite it being one of the main Indian religions, along with Buddhism, Hinduism, and Jainism, it is little understood in the US. Case in point: Growing up, if I saw someone wearing a turban, I instantly linked them with terrorism (a misunderstanding that was especially widespread following the terror attacks of 9/11). But when I went to Amritsar in northwestern India, the birthplace of Sikhism, I learned about the Sikh articles of faith, one of which is uncut hair. Both men and women of the Sikh faith may cover their hair with a turban, and turbans are an important part of their identity. In America (and at various times, across Western culture), the turban has been demonized, but really, the turban is a beautiful symbol of harmony. The Sikh religion rejects any social distinctions that lead to inequality and is so incredibly peaceful. The Golden Temple, the main landmark and meeting place in Amritsar, offers 100,000 free meals every day for anyone to come and enjoy. The Sikhs are pure souls.

Even when it comes to lesser-known religions (Voodooism, Rastafarianism, the Bahá'í Faith, Zoroastrianism, I could go on), they, too, are all steeped in peace and community, in love and connection. It is never the believers that want war with their neighbors but rather their governments that drive the divides between them, turning neighbors against each other.

REMEMBER, GOVERNMENTS ARE NOT PEOPLE

I'll say it again—GOVERNMENTS ARE NOT PEOPLE. So many countries out there are misconceived and misunderstood, but once you get there and meet the people, it feels like the exact opposite of what we've been told or what is true about their political leaders. People are not their politicians—just as we are not our politicians in the US. And thank goodness! I don't agree with everything that the government does, and I'm sure you don't either. (As an aside, it's sad how when we travel as Americans, we are judged in light of whoever is president at the time. During the Obama years, it was great to be an American abroad because he was so well liked around the world. During Trump's presidency, it was the exact opposite.) Most people are all just trying to live their lives, and those lives often don't look different from our own.

And sometimes this surprise can turn a trip you were concerned about into one of the greatest adventures of your life. And this is why I love Iran. Up until recently, with the understandable increase in protests after Mahsa Amini was killed for not wearing a hijab in public, Iran has been an incredibly safe country to visit and is home to the friendliest people on this planet. Most people on the street aren't religious, despite being ruled by an "Islamic government." On my first visit to Iran, it was Ramadan, and about 90 percent of the Iranians that I met were not fasting.

The Iranian people are a modern, educated, practically secular people, who participate in school and work and fun much like us. And their country is beautiful, but they also struggle under a dictatorship that doesn't reflect them or their views.

Governments are not the same as the local population. You have to give the people a chance and stop listening to the news. Going into places with an open mind and an open heart will really show you the people behind the politics. (To be clear: governments do need to exist, but they should represent their people, not create systems of oppression over them.)

ACCESS TO EDUCATION

Beyond governments, education has a large impact on how any given society is run. By improving education worldwide, we can help solve a lot of the world's biggest issues, such as poverty. It's important to recognize that education doesn't always have to be shared in a traditional classroom setting. Something as simple as having internet access—which many Americans take for granted—would make a drastic improvement in educating people. Having a smartphone and access to YouTube is a total game changer. Just take a look at the world's richest countries, which have the highest rate of smartphone use and the highest levels of education—South Korea, USA, Japan, Australia, Denmark. As you travel to these nations, you can see how advanced they are and how education (among other factors) has a positive impact of the country's progressiveness.

When you go to those countries where fewer people use smartphones, you can see how that really does impact the way society works and the efficiency of getting things done (going to the supermarket, going to the bank, going to the airport, going to the doctor, etc.). These simple tasks take a VERY LONG TIME in these countries, whereas they are a breeze in others.

I once was in Zambia, driving across the country with a hired driver. We pulled over at a checkpoint and we were caught up for about an hour by the police. While we were waiting for them to verify my passport and my visa, I met a guy on the side of the dirt road who was on his hands and knees fixing bike tires. I asked him how he got so talented and knowledgeable about fixing bikes, and he said that he taught himself everything from watching YouTube videos.

He told me that before he had a smartphone, he wasn't working and had no income. All of a sudden, he is making more money than all of his friends and doing something that is helping the local economy.

Everyone in this world has potential—they just need access to resources like education and technology in order to find their purpose and a means to survive. Consider this about education: In developing, low-income countries, every year that someone goes to school will increase their future income by 10 percent, on average. And yet, despite this, many of these same nations struggle with 50 percent literacy rates (by comparison, youth literacy in South America and Europe is around 90–100 percent), and in many of the same countries, sixty-one million school-age children were not enrolled in school.

Education matters. And having access to the internet matters.

Whether it's happening in formal school or informally on the internet, education is critical for all of us to expand our knowledge, our skills, and our opportunities to advance in this world, whether you're living in Kabul or Kansas City. The same is true for us all.

In fact, an estimated 37 percent of the world's population still has never used the internet. If we solved this problem, then these 2.9 billion people could learn anything they want via their fingertips.

Three of the Least Understood Countries in the World

MYANMAR

If you've ever been to Myanmar, then you'll know how incredible and peaceful it can be. It's like Thailand was in the 1970s, before it became overly developed. The people are so nice and they're always smiling.

Sadly, there is an ongoing (as of this writing) genocide of the Muslim Rohingya people by the military of Myanmar. There are killings daily and the country has been closed off to the public. I hear people judging the country based on these headlines, and it really is unfortunate. I'm thinking, *How could this happen in a country like Myanmar? What about all of the innocent people there?* It's heartbreaking that people judge the country because of what they hear on the news.

MEXICO

In Mexico, some American gets kidnapped while on vacation, and all of a sudden, everyone in the US (including my mom) is scared to visit Mexico. Complete nonsense. Though there are certainly areas with high rates of violence, there is also, sadly, often a difference between being a tourist and a resident of a certain area. Whereas violence or crime might plague a certain neighborhood on a regular basis, as a visitor, you might visit that area for only a couple of hours or not at all. And Mexico is one of the top ten most interesting countries in the world. It's amazing. It's huge. It's full of culture, food, things to do, and places to go. Mexico is not only its beaches—in fact, the farther away you get from the beaches in Mexico, the more interesting it gets, all the way down to Chiapas. Head to my favorite region, Oaxaca, the foodie capital of Mexico, or venture to Mexico City—where you can get lost in the markets and ancient wonders—and you will see how wonderful it is!

AFGHANISTAN

In chapter five, I told you about how much I loved my experiences in Afghanistan. But Afghanistan has been the recipient of a lot of prejudice ever since 9/11, and sadly, is now being run by the Taliban. The forty million people in Afghanistan are NOT the Taliban. Those terrorists make up 1 percent of the country. And I would argue that even many of those in the Taliban aren't terrible people; they are just sucked into the system.

It's really sad that tourism is basically shut off indefinitely because of the current situation. Afghanistan is a wildly stunning country inside and out, from the snowy mountains of Bamiyan to the Friday mosque of Herat to the bustling markets in Kabul to the pomegranate farms in Kandahar. Every time I think of Afghanistan, a smile comes to my face when reminiscing on my time spent traveling the country. I hope to return as soon as it becomes safer.

EXPECT THE UNEXPECTED

On October 21, 2021, I set foot in the 197th and final country on my list—Saudi Arabia.

Though by that point I knew that I'd be surprised by what I'd find, I couldn't help but let the news color my perspective. What we hear about Saudi Arabia is that it is a country of extremes: extreme laws, extreme hate crimes, extreme punishments, extreme human rights issues. And I am not going to say that any of these things are false. In fact, much of it is true. (And that doesn't mean I could just ignore the human rights violations— but more on that later in this chapter.) Still, like everywhere else, it is also a country rich in culture and humor and joy.

Before I went to Saudi Arabia, I expected a lot of poverty, dirt roads, unfinished buildings, people who were only speaking Arabic, and women who were completely covered up from head to toe. But after going there, I saw something else.

I landed in Jeddah, and I have never been happier than that moment of getting off the plane. It didn't hit me until I walked in the bathroom, looked in the mirror, and I was like, *Holy shit . . . That is the face of a guy who has just completed his lifelong goal to visit every single country in this entire planet.* I was hit with a massive wave of press in my hotel room: CNN, Bloomberg, the *New York Times*, ABC News, and Fox. It was a blast. But I still didn't know what to expect from this upcoming two-week journey that I had planned. I was traveling with my documentary producer/director, Chris Wedding; my content-creator friend, Uptin; and a cinematographer, Randy.

We were all a little nervous but excited to explore one of the world's biggest countries and the birthplace of Islam.

I was greeted right away by my local friend from Jeddah, Sarah, who is a popular Arabic traveler and Instagrammer. She runs her own travel tour company, and she was actually the one who picked me up at the airport in her car. That was my first impression of Saudi Arabia, a young woman picking me up in her car—driving—without wearing a hijab. It wasn't what I expected from Saudi Arabia. It felt more like Dubai. Or even Arizona.

As the days went on, I quickly realized that Saudis tend to be highly educated. Many Saudis have a higher education through university, and many go beyond—men and woman alike. Lots of Saudis speak perfect English, and everything is extremely modern and fancy. Jeddah is a melting pot of people and culture because of nearby Mecca, the touchstone of Islam. There are a lot of people over the years who have gone on pilgrimages from nearby nations—East Africa, Yemen, Pakistan, Bangladesh, Afghanistan, Iran, and more—and never left. Because of this, the food is diverse and amazing. But, perhaps most surprisingly to me, Saudi Arabia felt like a liberal, open-minded place.

The people spoke openly about their government, their political opinions, and their religious beliefs. I could have been anywhere in America the way young people socialized, treating each other like equals, even if they might behave differently in more traditional settings.

And the beaches in Jeddah blew me away. Talk about crystal-clear blue water and a lovely boardwalk that is lined with cafés, restaurants, shisha places, and more.

"I told you that we have many surprises here!" Sarah exclaimed.

"It's insane!!" I replied. "This beauty of this place reminds me of Zanzibar or the Philippines! Is this really Saudi Arabia?!"

This beach was just the start of an epic two weeks ahead with Sarah. We drove, we chatted, we ate, we went to the countryside, we explored big cities—and Saudi Arabia is beautiful.

It's the home of hospitality and it's the birthplace of Islam. As I've discovered, the two go hand in hand. Because if you've been to a Muslim-majority country before, then you know that their people are well known to be the most hospitable in the world.

We went from Jeddah to Riyadh (the capital) to Jazan in the south, right by the Yemeni border. It was fascinating to see the similarities of the cultures between Saudi and Yemen. We made our way up to AlUla national park, which is like a more surreal version of Petra and Jordan, with ancient rock formations built into the tombs on the cliffs. Half natural, half man-made.

For a couple of nights, we stayed with a very remote Bedouin tribe, who were living in the desert and herding their camels in the same way that their ancestors have done for thousands of years. What an amazing experience that was. I really felt in my element in Saudi Arabia, going around the country and filming people, all of whom were so open to share and talk about their cultures, including the preconceived notions that Westerners have about them and the way they live.

As Sarah explained, "You know, at one point, everyone in Saudi Arabia lived like this. This was their life. Desert and camels and lots of tea and laughter. It's a shame that my country gets such a bad rep in the Western media because we are just normal people who are enjoying life. And you are now seeing it with your own eyes."

As I've said, the people are not a representation of the government. Time and time again, I see that this is true. I do disagree with Saudi politics, in the same way that I disagree with many other countries' politics, but the local people are just wonderful. They're hardworking folks who deserve a chance. Just like me and you, they need to make money to have a roof over their heads, and they need to exercise to stay in shape and they need to love and be loved in return.

RECOGNIZE THAT HUMAN RIGHTS ISSUES ARE EVERYWHERE (EVEN IN AMERICA)

I don't want to ignore the human rights issues in Saudi Arabia, such as a potential death penalty for LGBTQ+ people and limitations on freedoms for women in the country, especially those from less-resourced communities.

> **Part of travel is learning to tweeze apart the politics of a country from the people who live there.**

But also, many, if not most, countries have human rights abuses, including America. Sure, there are some anomalies like Iceland and Luxembourg (perhaps?). In these places, you will likely find the lowest percentage of human rights violations. On the other hand, you have countries like Mauritania, where slavery is still happening and people are being killed left and right. In extremist countries, like Afghanistan for example, there are genocides among the Hazara people who are being killed for their Asian appearance. The Jews have been attacked around the world for centuries. The Iranian government is killing women in the streets for not covering their hair. In China, more than two million Uyghurs, the Chinese Muslims who reside in the western provinces, have been killed. We could also talk about the US and all the wars that we've been involved in, and how many deaths we've been responsible for. We could talk about Russia, Turkey, Ethiopia, not to mention Israel and Palestine.

Saudi Arabia is no different. There are certainly problems there, and we constantly hear about them in the news. Mass media can establish a preconceived perspective of what life is like in these countries, without really going there to see the reality with our own eyes.

The point is, we know that human rights issues are everywhere. Racism is everywhere. So are rape, murder, drugs, guns, etc. And sadly, I don't see a world in the near future where that stuff goes away. But that being said, it's in my best interest as a content creator to also share the good side of humanity. To focus on the positives. Why would I focus on the negative when there's so much positivity going on in the world? If you want to hear about the negatives, I'll give you the TV remote and you can turn on CNN or Fox or MSNBC to learn about all the terrible things happening in the world.

I sincerely believe in giving everybody a chance and a voice on my platform. And that leads me into the next point for why we shouldn't judge a country by its worst stories. Being open-minded is so important. The best stories happen when you allow yourself to be vulnerable!

On one evening in Jazan, Saudi Arabia, I was walking around the market and got lost (without my friends). We were just a few miles away from the Yemeni border, so things felt a bit tense with police cars and security monitoring the area. A group of young men in their early twenties pulled up to me in a pickup truck and said to me in Arabic, "Are you lost? Can I help you?" which I was able to translate by context.

"I'm all right, just looking for my friends!" I said, nervous despite their kindness.

They ended up getting out of their car and waiting with me until my friends showed up, which happened to be about fifteen minutes later. They even offered to drive me to my hotel, should nobody be there to find me.

It's little moments like this that go a long way in proving that the world is safer than we think—and we need to look past the outside, and unlearn what we think we know, to really appreciate its people.

📍 Ashgabat, Turkmenistan

CHAPTER 8

Be Grateful

I want to turn your attention to a country that means a lot to me and a culture that I think about every day. The country of Syria.

In some ways, Syria can be considered as the pinnacle of travel (especially among hard-core travelers and those of us who are going to every country in the world). The visa situation alone is daunting. I had to enter Syria on a volunteer visa because tourist visas are not issued to any American citizen. And I was lucky to get the volunteer visa!

It wasn't an easy country to visit, but it was one of the easiest countries to love. I really connected with this Middle Eastern land that few outsiders get the chance to see. Syrian people were the first to show me what true kindness and hospitality are all about. I walked away after a two-week trip in Syria with an immense feeling of gratitude for being able to experience all of its glory. Even during times of war, I was still able to connect with the people and learn about the amazing history of the region, which is where humans first settled and learned to farm.

And it showed me that by learning about what others have gone through, we come home understanding why we have to care about each other; our humanity depends on it.

ASK QUESTIONS AND REALLY LISTEN

It was a brisk autumn morning, about 45°F, which was a lot colder than I expected or was prepared for, but it didn't matter. I was beyond excited to be in Syria's vibrant capital of Damascus. After a stressful day crossing the border from Lebanon, I had actually gotten a good night's sleep and now I was hitting the streets of Damascus with my new friend and local tour guide, Ghaidaa. I was introduced to her by my buddy Alvaro, who had hired her as a guide a few months prior. Ghaidaa is about my age, and that morning she was wearing a black hijab and a smile that could brighten any room. Damascus was beautiful and awake and alive despite its recent history, but nothing caught my eye more than its bustling markets. Seemingly on every corner, there was another butcher, craftsman, or street vendor selling some kind of unique product made from hand and from the heart.

As we were strolling down a side street, a small, hole-in-the-wall shop caught my eye. I noticed two elderly men through the window who seemed to be working hard on making something by hand. Both men were wearing gray collared shirts, open-buttoned at the top, and they each had comb-overs to cover up their receding hairlines. The younger of the two men had a gray mustache, while the other was freshly shaven. As soon as I walked in, getting a huge whiff of freshly shaved wood, I was greeted with two massive smiles.

"Hello and welcome inside our mosaic store," exclaimed the older fellow.

"Thank you very much," I murmured, still a bit nervous—I'd only been in Syria for a few hours. They led me to their back room where their finished products were displayed for purchase. Every piece was handcrafted and beautifully presented. I had never seen art like that before in my life. Every design was made from polished wood, crafted into tables, chairs, plates, cabinets, chess sets, and beyond. I instantly bought a small jewelry box for Deanna.

As he rang up my purchase, Ibrahim, the younger of the two, began to describe their work. "We make mosaics for seventy years in this store. Would you like some hot tea?"

"Sure, I'd love that," I said with a big smile, still warming up on this surprisingly cold morning. As we enjoyed a delicious glass of sweet tea, a Syrian specialty, Ghaidaa translated for us. I told Antonio and Ibrahim that it was my very first day in Syria, and that I was on a mission to visit every country in the world. Syria was country #183. I explained that I create travel videos and documentaries about people and culture and asked if they wanted to be interviewed for a story. Their faces lit up immediately.

"Please take our photo," said Antonio, pointing to the wall of a photo of him and his brother. Within seconds, the scene basically turned into a photo shoot, and I couldn't have been happier. All of the fear, anxiety, and skepticism that I had before coming to Syria was eliminated the moment I walked through their door.

But as we began to talk more about their life in Syria, reality kicked in. During the worst years of Syria's war, around four years prior, Antonio and Ibrahim kept their shop open while all of their friends and family members fled the city and country. The two brothers worked every day in their shop to the sound of bombs and gunfire directly outside its walls.

As Ghaidaa translated, the brothers explained that they would run to their rooftop during the war, hiding from the gunfire. Ibrahim motioned his thumb and index finger into a gun.

"Wow," I said anxiously, unable to say anything else. The story they were telling felt like it should have been a distant memory and not something that had happened just a couple years before, not something that is still happening across their country.

Ibrahim noticed my reaction, again speaking through Ghaidaa. "My friend, don't be sad. The past is the past. We are strong people. Come with us and we will show you how we make mosaics."

I followed both men again to the back room, sitting down across from them as they put on their shiny goggles, took out a dusty hammer, and started crafting a piece of wood into the most amazing design. I didn't miss a beat, filming everything that they were doing, knowing this was going to be a special story for the world to see.

One of the most important reasons to capture the moments of travel is to hold on to experiences you might never see again—and which you can share with people who might never see them either.

One of the guys took out a bottle of alcohol. "Do you like drink?"

"No thanks, I am okay," I said, thinking it was illegal to drink alcohol in Syria.

Ibrahim laughed, sensing my hesitation. "We are not Muslim. We are Christian. Drinking no problem for us. We have many bars and clubs in Damascus."

I had no idea that it was legal to drink in Syria. I just assumed that it was a dry country like its neighbors of Iran, Afghanistan, and Saudi Arabia. But as I quickly discovered, 10 percent of Syrians are Christians, and they own dozens of bars that line the streets of Damascus's old city.

As I said goodbye to Antonio and Ibrahim later that day, I couldn't help but be amazed at how quickly humans can bond over a cup of tea (or a shot of alcohol), no matter where we come from or what might have happened to us.

Whenever you meet strangers, I always find it valuable to ask them simple questions such as: "What do you enjoy (or not enjoy) about living here?"

Or "What makes you happy (or stressed) in life?"

By asking them about their lives, their hobbies, the reasons they love or complain about their country, you begin to find out a lot more about the place you're visiting, but also, you connect with the people who live there, becoming friends, and making lifelong relationships that can change your life more than any selfie or visit to a monument.

RESPECT A COUNTRY'S HISTORY (ESPECIALLY IF IT JUST HAPPENED YESTERDAY)

Up until 2011, Syria was a tourist haven. Millions of people came from all corners of the world to witness life in the cradle of civilization—to experience a beautiful Mediterranean coastline, to eat some delicious Middle Eastern food, to visit two-thousand-year-old ancient ruins, and to enjoy some of the world's finest hospitality.

But that all changed, less the hospitality, after the Arab Spring kicked off in early 2011. The series of anti-governmental protests, uprisings, and armed rebellions—in response to oppressive regimes and low standards of living—first erupted in Tunisia and then quickly spread across much of the Arab world, most notably in Libya, Egypt, Yemen, and Syria. In Syria, they grew out of discontent with that nation's government and quickly escalated to an armed conflict after protests for the removal of Syria's president Bashar al-Assad were violently suppressed.

Soon after, things turned for the worse inside this Middle Eastern nation. A proxy war broke out between major international world powers, including Iran, Russia, Turkey, and the United States, not to mention several others. That war grew into one of the greatest humanitarian crises in modern history. A United Nations agency estimates that the war in Syria has cost the country over $450 billion USD in economic damage.

Entering its ninth year of conflict, more than half a million Syrians have been killed and more than a million others have been injured. About half of Syria's twelve million residents have left their homes for safety, crossing into Europe, Lebanon, Egypt, Jordan, Iraq, and Turkey, and causing a massive refugee crisis in their forced exodus.

Today, all across Syria, you can see remnants of buildings that were destroyed. Fresh bullet holes mark the city walls. Ancient wonders have been turned to rubble. Complete neighborhoods, grand mosques, schools, and stadiums have all been left in pieces. But the culture remains. It was why I was so determined to go to Syria, no matter how hard it might be to get in.

That said, as I walked around Damascus, it was sometimes hard to believe what it had gone through in the years just prior. Much of the city is still intact. Damascus is known to be the oldest continuously inhabited city in the world, and every corner tells a story of who we are, who we have been, and how long humans have endured. On one of my last days in the city before leaving to tour the rest of the country, I visited the Umayyad Mosque, which was converted from a church and is considered to be the fourth most important mosque in the world of Islam.

Ghaidaa and I went inside. Traditionally, women aren't allowed to walk with men in mosques; they must go through a separate entrance for women only. Ghaidaa explained to the security guard that she was my tour guide and translator, and he allowed her into the area that was usually only reserved for men. The mosque has remained unchanged for thousands of years, and as Ghaidaa and I walked through it, it seemed that we could hear the walls talking to us, whispering the secrets of this country that has at once been the cradle of human civilization, the heart of the Middle East, the tourist haven, and now, after years of war, rising back to life. Through a friend, Ghaidaa was able to get us access to the rooftop.

Together, we climbed one of the narrowest staircases I have walked, finally emerging on top of the mosque, looking out at the city and the land beyond. There was only room for one on the balcony, so Ghaidaa and I took turns. I stood out, gazing across the city, across our history, and I couldn't have been more grateful to Ghaidaa for the moment. I was the only foreigner to have ever been given access to the view, offering me a taste of Damascus that few have experienced.

Because no matter the war, as I looked out at Damascus, I could feel the city coming back—the tourist haven, the heart of the Middle East, the cradle of human civilization.

It's important to read up on the current political/safety situation in a country before going there, and then from experience being on the ground, you will learn so much more that will boost your knowledge and help you better understand the reality of a place like Syria.

UNDERSTAND YOUR PRIVILEGE

For years, all of the airports in Syria had been closed to commercial flights. The only way to get into that nation was to fly to Lebanon and cross the border by car.

Lebanon happens to be one of my top ten favorite countries in the world, so I was thrilled to go back. I have a couple of good Lebanese friends, Georgio and Olivia, who I always stay with in Beirut. When I got to Georgio's house, he couldn't believe that I was going to Syria.

"My mom would never let me go there," he said. "It's too dangerous."

I began to rethink my decision to go. What if something went wrong? What if nobody heard from me again? What if I got kidnapped? If my Lebanese friends were telling me all of these things and they live just across the border, then what do I know?

This is where our American naiveté can sometimes serve us or fail us. I know that my passport can create complications, but generally, on the ground, being an American male has allowed me access to places others might not have been comfortable visiting. Sometimes, not knowing is the best defense, because I don't come with a set of politics or opinion. I don't try to convince or convert. I just try to be a good student, and in that curiosity, typically, the other person's defenses also come down. I hoped that my not knowing would serve me in Syria.

The overwhelming majority of travelers that come to Syria stay in and around Damascus, so when I had the chance to see places that nobody had visited in years, I jumped. Traveling with a nongovernmental organization (NGO) that was hosting me, we took a small bus to the coast. Syria has a long Mediterranean coastline and is home to some of the most beautiful beaches in the region. Much of this area was off-limits but has recently reopened to visitors, and we were some of the first to go.

Our first stop was the coastal city of Latakia. It was lunchtime and we rolled up to a restaurant on the hill, overlooking the deep blue sea. It was the most modern restaurant I had been to in the past three months. The restaurant was like eating at the Ritz-Carlton, with the waiters wearing tuxes and bow ties. I had forgotten that just ten years prior, this region had been like the Riviera of the Middle East, where the wealthy from Jordan, Lebanon, and Syria would congregate in summer, eating, drinking (for those who did), and dancing by the sea. It would be like visiting Miami after ten years of war if the restaurants and hotels still remained.

After lunch, we walked down the hill to a pier, where there were some older men fishing and enjoying the sunshine. One of the fishermen, who was probably in his fifties and wearing a blue scrappy shirt, noticed my camera.

He approached me, speaking in the most perfect English accent I'd heard in the country so far: "Hello there. How are you doing?"

He shared that he had only caught one fish that day but was working to get more.

"Your English is really good," I told him. "How did you learn?"

"My brother lives in Chicago and I visit him often," he explained. "I love America. It's a great country."

Though it's happened across the world so many times, I am always surprised to find how many people have visited the United States, journeying across the world to work, to visit family, to see the place they have only seen in movies, and then they return home, even if home is being torn apart by war or poverty.

Because home is always home. |

As he told me about *his* travels, I felt like I was hanging out with one of my friends back home. He interrupted our conversation to invite me for a cup of tea, and we chatted more about America and his favorite things about my own home.

"You're the first American I've seen in ten years," and though his eyes darkened at the statement, we didn't talk about the war or politics or any of the hard stories that had taken place in Syria in the last ten years. Instead, we just got to know one another outside of the differences of our two nations.

For a moment, we shared a common understanding—what it means to be home.

As we left Latakia, I couldn't help but think of my own country. What would it feel like to go from living a normal life, where we feel safe out on the streets, where we travel freely and eat at our fancy restaurants, where we eat and drink and dance by the sea, and then almost overnight see our way of life disappear? It was November 2019, and I didn't realize how much was about to change in the world. But as we drove away from that seaside town, I understood that no matter what, our humanity remains.

My Four Favorite Things About the Middle East

The Middle East is my favorite region in the world for many reasons (yes, even as a white, Jewish American!), but none more than the hospitality. From Iran to Lebanon, Jordan, Israel, Palestine, Egypt, and Turkey, I am always overwhelmed by how kind everyone is in this part of the world. I had somewhat expected that Syrians would be the same, but I really underestimated to what extent.

THE PEOPLE

Over the course of fifteen days, I traveled from Damascus to Homs, Aleppo, Latakia, Tartus, Maaloula, Mhardeh, and Sadad. Despite the images and horror stories those names might conjure for some, I didn't meet a single person who was unfriendly or unwelcoming. I was invited into homes to sleep and into restaurants for free meals. One lady I met in the small village of Mhardeh insisted that I sleep in her bed, choosing instead to sleep on her own floor. People who I met for the first time were giving me gifts for no apparent reason other than sheer kindness. I had to purchase an extra suitcase just to bring everything home. It was worth paying the extra bag (and overweight fee), because now I proudly display these items in my office at home.

THE MARKETS

As I strolled through the colorful markets of Damascus, countless street vendors offered me a free meal while putting a hand over their heart. This is a customary thing that Arabs do to show their respect and love, and I experienced it more in Syria than anywhere else. Even if English is not widely spoken or understood, I still had dozens of people (both young and old) approach me on the streets just to say hi and "Welcome to Syria." Every city that I went to in that country was centered around a busy marketplace, where you can find all things from street food to electronics to antiques to home goods—and the quality of products are great for a low price! Even if you don't buy anything, just walking through and looking around, or using your sense of smell to guide you to the best vendors, is truly a blast.

THE FOOD

Ah, where to start? Syrian food is among the world's best. It's the birthplace of hummus, falafel, kibbeh, and shawarma—some of the all-time best dishes in the world! Syria is blessed with an abundance of fresh fruits and vegetables, due to the variety of climates, so therefore, you can find excellent fruit juices, pastries, and desserts. All throughout the Middle East, there are fresh, delicious, inexpensive meals that feel like they were made with joy and love—even in the toughest of conditions. If there's any one thing that is pulling me back to visit Syria—it is the cuisine.

THE FAITH

Syria (and the Middle East as a whole) is a very spiritual place. And not only in regard to Islam. In Syria, for example, about 10 percent of the population are Christians, and you can see touches of this around the country—there is even a Christian Quarter in Damascus where you can get any beer you want! Given its close proximity to Jerusalem, you can really feel the essence of a higher being looking over you, unlike any other place that you will go. The Middle East is pure magic, and the only way to really experience it is by booking your flight!

APPRECIATE WHAT OTHERS HAVE EXPERIENCED

We arrived in Sadad on a Wednesday morning. I had only a week left in the trip, and I was already mourning my departure. Over the last two weeks, I had found a home in Syria. There are places I have visited where I might learn a lot about the culture, but I always felt like a visitor, looking in from the outside. But not here. I connected to the Syrian people simply through their openness, through their deep love for the world.

I wonder whether facing such pain forces people to live in the present. You can't be bothered with silly worries and unnecessary concerns. The stakes have been raised so high that every day you wake up alive is its own deep celebration.

Sadad is a sleepy, Christian town of no more than eight thousand residents, located in the middle of the Syrian desert. We arrived around 10 AM, just as the heat was beginning to settle in. The town is painted in shades of brown, from the sandy ground to the various churches to the makeshift buildings. I was traveling again with the NGO, who suggested I meet with the former mayor of the town, who had become famous for his heroism in the war.

We rolled up to the man's house, which was more like a palace, and knocked on the door. A man appeared with a huge smile on his young face.

"Welcome to Syria," he greeted us with the common refrain in the country. "And welcome to Sadad. My name is Suliman."

Suliman was short, about my height at five foot seven. He was wearing a collared shirt, and he had dark-brown hair that was spiked up in the front, similar to my hairstyle in high school. Sometimes it's these small cultural similarities that create the strongest connection. Because even though we might live on opposite sides of the world, we wear the same brands, we share the same hairstyles, we mirror each other even if we have very different lives.

Suliman invited us in, and I quickly found out that, much like my fisherman friend, Suliman had also spent some time in America.

"I spent nine years living in the United States, working," he explained. "I love your country—land of the free, home of the brave."

As brave as I might think my native country is, I couldn't imagine a braver people than the Syrians, and as Suliman told me of his experience during the war, he might be one of the bravest.

"I was the mayor of Sadad from 2013 to 2015," he told me but then laughed slightly. "I did everything but be a mayor. I was more of a military leader."

He explained how Sadad ended up being the first Christian town to defeat ISIS. As he shared: "They came into our town and occupied it for a week, killing forty-four innocent people. I quickly gathered a militia, and we fought them back. I gathered men, trained them, gave them salaries and weapons, and had them protect our town of eight thousand people. And we won."

He sat back in his chair proudly. No matter what I had accomplished in life, it was hard to believe that this man, who didn't look much older than me, wearing my hairstyle from high school and a Tommy Hilfiger shirt, had been responsible for defeating ISIS.

"What was that like?" I asked.

He reached over behind his head to a red curtain in front of the window, pulling back the curtain. "Look at that, do you see that?"

"No, what is it?"

"Those are bullet holes," he explained. "They came on my property and were shooting at me and my family, especially in my mother's room next door."

As I looked around the room, I realized that the walls were covered in bullet holes, at least fifteen to twenty that I could count. I had gotten so comfortable sitting in Suliman's living room, it felt like we were just sitting in my house in Arizona, not in the middle of a war zone.

It can be overwhelming to understand the violence that wreaks havoc over our world, but that overwhelm is often softened by the humanity that surges in opposition.

"Did you ever think that you were going to die?" I asked him, comfortable enough to do so.

"Actually, it's the feeling like you are walking dead," he said. "You don't make those differences; I mean between death and life. Listen, when the bullet passes next to your head, you hear a loud whistle. I always tell my men to feel happy when you hear that sound . . . because that means you're still alive. It's the bullet that hits you that you don't hear."

And that is Syrian gratitude. Instead of being lost to the grief of the bullet, they are grateful for every moment they are alive. They know how precious life is because they have faced death, forced to confront every day not knowing if it would be their last. Though the peace there is tenuous, and war still rages in some regions, the relative calm they have experienced in recent years has quickly reconnected them into the country they once were: known for their humor and hospitality, for their beautiful cites and coastal towns.

They are not quite free yet, but they are brave. And they are looking toward the future with a hope we all should try to share.

Because it's easy to get caught up in the conflicts of our country (even the ones that are much less violent and scary than other countries), but home is home. And as I learned in Syria, home is also hope.

On my final evening in Syria, I found myself back in Damascus with Ghaidaa. Ironically, it was Thanksgiving Day back in the US, and although they obviously don't celebrate that American holiday in Syria (and they don't eat turkey), I was still able to celebrate. Ghaidaa told me that her colleague, Fadi, wanted to invite me over to his house for a home-cooked meal. They were going to make kibbeh—which is my favorite Syrian dish. I joined them in the early morning to pick up all of the ingredients in the market.

I kept offering to pay for food, but Fadi kept putting the money back in my pocket. Once again, this is Syrian hospitality at its finest.

We arrived at Fadi's house on the outskirts of Damascus, some forty minutes away from downtown. We had to cross two police checkpoints to get there, but after showing my passport, everything was okay. As soon as we arrived at Fadi's apartment complex, we were greeted by his wife and daughter, who made me feel immediately at home. The two women went inside to start preparing the food, while I sat outside with Fadi and Ghaidaa to chat.

After three hours, the house started to smell like paradise. Kibbeh is the national dish of Syria, but it's also popular over the border in Lebanon, where I've tried it many times. The word translates to "the shape of a ball," and it consists of dough made of meat, mixed with onions and spices, and formed into football-shaped croquettes. Then, it's filled with more minced meat, onions, pine nuts, and spices before being deep-fried to perfection. The dish is served crispy on the outside and soft on the inside. It is probably the only dish that can give Thanksgiving turkey a run for its money (at least, in my opinion).

Fadi invited his relatives over, and there were about ten of us at the dinner table, speaking in English and Arabic, but all smiling and laughing in the same language. Though I missed my family so much, I couldn't have been more grateful. My time in Syria wasn't about visiting a war-torn country, it was about discovering just how brave and resilient people can be.

> **No matter what happens out there on the streets, no matter the bombs or bullets, no one can stop humans from connecting, laughing at the same joke, wearing the same shirt, loving the same food, knowing that no matter how different our lives might look, we are deeply and thankfully very much the same.**

When we finished, I offered once more to pay for the meal, but Fadi insisted that I put my wallet away. "We don't accept money from visitors," he said. "So, you must come back!"

As I drove back across the Syrian border, returning to Lebanon, I felt like a different person than I was just two weeks before. I felt connection and understanding.

I will never forget something that Ghaidaa told me when we visited a nearby village outside of Damascus. As we were sitting on top of a mountain that we had just hiked, overlooking the city, she explained, "Every Syrian person knows someone directly who lost their lives in this war. It's our fathers, our aunts, our cousins, our classmates, and our colleagues. After a bombing or a terrorist attack, we all know the feeling of picking up the phone and calling our loved ones to see if they are still alive. But despite living through the worst crisis in modern history, somehow we have hope. Syrians are the strongest, most resilient people in the world. And we're ready to move forward to a better tomorrow."

After hearing her words, I wondered why these bad things happened to innocent Syrians and not to me? Tears came to my eyes. Why was my life so good? I began to feel this immense sensation of gratitude. Grateful to be from a country that is safe. Grateful to have all of my friends, family members, and loved ones alive. Grateful to have the opportunity to travel and visit places like Syria to learn about new cultures. Grateful to have the ability to document everything and inspire people to learn about the world.

And finally, grateful to know that there are so many amazing souls existing in Syria and across the world. I look forward to seeing them again soon.

Be Spontaneous

I wouldn't be writing this book if I was not spontaneous.

On my study abroad program in Prague back in 2012, I showed up without knowing a single person. I packed my bags and moved seven thousand miles across the world, and I had no idea what I was getting into. However, it turned out to be the best five months of my life. Even on my trip to Prague ten years later, I showed up without even a hotel reservation. In fact, most of the time I visit a new city, I don't even book a hotel before I arrive. Look, I understand this might be hard and

PART THREE

📍 Prague, Czech Republic

sometimes even impossible for some travelers to do (especially if you need special travel arrangements), but 197 countries later, I've never once failed to find a place to sleep. And the more you learn to be spontaneous (when you can), the more you will learn about the world. I've traveled with people who plan activities from 7 AM until 10 PM, and that takes all of the fun out of it. And to be honest, I get really stressed when things are overplanned. It's way more enjoyable to go with the flow because it always ends up working out in the end. Always.

📍 Bagan, Myanmar

CHAPTER 9

The Five Rules of Spontaneity

Recently, I went on my honeymoon with Deanna (that's right, over the course of this book, she went from fiancée to wife!). Because we're not your usual pair of travelers, our honeymoon travel list looked a little different than the usual trip to Hawaii or even Paris. Instead, we went to Uzbekistan, Rwanda, Ethiopia, DR Congo, Dubai, and Saudi Arabia. And we went with only a few plans and no schedule; it was so much fun! The only things we had planned were flights (and some hotels), and the rest of the trip we just figured out as went. The best moments were meeting the Pygmy tribe in the middle of the jungle, exploring the ancient city of Harar (Ethiopia), meeting the man who feeds wild hyenas every night from his front porch, and skydiving over the man-made Palm Islands of Dubai. And guess what, none of these things were planned until the day of!

I know that many people (including Deanna—which is why some hotels were booked in advance) need some parameters in place to feel safe and to know what's happening next, but as I always say, the best moments in life happen from being spontaneous. And when you are going to a new place, you lose out on so many opportunities by not letting the place take you on a ride.

There is nothing like surrendering to a new city, a new language, a new culture, and allowing it to shape your experience (and itinerary) when you're visiting a new place—rather than trying to make it your own.

The world is full of adventure, but in order to experience it, we have to be willing to be adventurous. We have to be willing to JUST GO!

(Even if you're on your honeymoon in Rwanda without a plan!)

RULE #1: ALWAYS SAY YES, UNLESS IT'S DANGEROUS

Well, you can say yes as long as it's not *too* dangerous, anyway. As you know from chapter four, I'm all in favor of taking risks when they're worth it—but safety does come first.

Do you want to hike up that mountain? Yes. Do you want to go to that bar across the street? Yes. Do you want to randomly approach a stranger on the road and ask him/her to join you for coffee? Yes. Life changes when you say yes more often. That's a scientific fact. I mean, don't ask me for research on it, but I have learned it on the road of life. Saying yes makes life more exciting. You will go to places that you never dreamed of going and meet people who you never expected to meet. When I look back at all of my favorite memories—skydiving in Australia, trekking across Myanmar, scuba diving in Palau—they all happened because I said yes.

One time in Syria, I was asked by a stranger if I wanted to go to the top of the Citadel of Aleppo, the oldest city in the world. The hike up looked a bit unsafe because of the destruction from the ISIS war, but I said yes. When I got to the top, I met the most incredible Syrian soldiers who were drinking black tea. They offered me a cup, and we shared stories together as we gazed at the best view of the city. I remember standing up, walking off to the side, and smiling as big as I could because who else could get an experience like that? It wasn't because I was special though.

It was simply because I said yes.

Of course, you should trust your gut instinct, and if something tells you to avoid the situation and walk away, then do that. But if you use common judgment and assess your surroundings and you feel like it's okay, then go for it!

RULE #2: DON'T LET YOUR ITINERARY DICTATE YOUR ADVENTURE

There is a time and a place for planning (especially if, say, you're jumping aboard an iron ore train or venturing into the world's more dangerous countries or cities). But there's also a time and a place to throw it out the window or leave your itinerary open.

In my early days of travel, I planned a lot. I had itineraries for each place I went, and I would check the boxes after I completed each activity. When I went to Myanmar in 2013, I showed up in Yangon with a plan. But then I met up with a friend of a friend, and she took me out to all of her favorite places. It's the same concept for why Airbnb is better than hotels—because you get that feeling of "living like a local."

During that trip to Myanmar, I didn't even go to the Shwedagon Pagoda, the main attraction of Yangon. I went to other, smaller pagodas, which were just as spectacular! I also skipped the big night market and went to a local one in her family's neighborhood. Eating street food at that market, without any other tourists in sight, was one of the most memorable moments of that trip. It's a great feeling to be thrown into a culture and observe how people are living their lives. They teach us what diversity truly means—that even though we might look different, or pray differently, or eat differently, we are all united.

On my next visit to Myanmar, in February 2020, I went back to Yangon, but I didn't enjoy it as much because I visited all of the main attractions like a normal tourist. It was when I went like a local that I truly learned and fell in love with the culture and people of Myanmar.

While being spontaneous is fun and my preferred way to travel, for others, it might be a good idea to have at least a general idea of what you want to do and how to get there, or you might end up missing out on the best things. Open up a notepad in your phone and write down as much as you can, assess the situation when you get there, and then give yourself the time and space to say yes to the unexpected.

RULE #3: LET THE LOCALS GUIDE YOU

In Kyoto, Japan, I met a guy named Haruto on the website Couchsurfing .com. I actually slept at his house for free (because that's how couch surfing works!). One morning, I was about to leave his house and walk around the city by foot, and he said to me, "You know what? You should take my extra bike, so you can visit all these different temples at your own pace. You'll enjoy the experience a lot more."

I borrowed his bike, and I had the most incredible time in Kyoto, Japan's most beautiful city. Haruto came with me, and together we explored the city, chatting along the way. If I close my eyes right now, I can remember riding around the city, going to Zen gardens and temples, and realizing, *Wow, I'm only doing this because my local friend told me to do it.* These little moments can make or break your experience in any place, in any country, in any city. You just have to trust your instinct. Put your faith in local people and realize that whatever they recommend is probably a better idea than what you could ever possibly imagine on your own. As they say, "Happiness is only real when shared," and I can confirm that it's true.

While traveling alone has its perks (to be able to do what you want, when you want), I think that traveling with a new local friend is way more rewarding. And then the next time you visit that city or country, you have someone to call (and vice versa, if they visit your hometown!).

If I hadn't listened to the locals, I never would have visited the Mesopotamian marshlands. They stretch 1,500 miles from southeastern Iraq to southwestern Iran. It's a UNESCO World Heritage Site, and I only heard about it because my friend and I followed the locals' advice to go there. And as someone who has experienced the Arctic at dawn and the Amazon at dusk, it was still one of the most incredible places I have been. It feels like a world removed from our own, set back in time, but also, in its own way, like it's a place from the future.

It is the home of the marsh Arabs—an entire population who only get around by boat. Yes—there aren't roads or cars, only a massive system of streams where locals take small boats to work, trade, live, visit, and thrive. Their livelihood consists of catching seafood known as "masgouf." They sing songs and have shisha parties under the moonlight. Some forty thousand people live down there in the marshlands—the main town is Chibayish. It's seriously one of the most surreal places that I've been to in the world, and once again, I would have never discovered it if I had a jam-packed day-to-day itinerary.

On my second day in the marshlands, I met a local, friendly, elderly man named Abu Haidar, who had a long gray beard and a red turban on his head. He guided me around his remote little fishing village, which had a few huts constructed from palm trees, with holes in the ground for making fire, and about a dozen water buffalo grazing around the humid swamps. Before dinner, I watched him as he washed his hands in the river and prayed. I admired how he caught the Iraqi freshwater fish, masgouf, and cooked it right there in a makeshift fireplace next to me. I'm talking about delicious, tender, tasty, white-meat fish. Abu Haidar taught me about the history of his tribe—how they herd water buffalo and care for their neighbors. Even as recent as the nineties, when Saddam Hussein was president and drained all of the marshlands to try to force people to move, Abu Haidar survived.

Its people were determined to keep their culture intact—living in the waters, creating homes among the marshes. I woke up at dawn to the sounds of birds I had never heard before and watched the sun go down as the men sang their ancient songs, reminding me that if we don't take our chances, we might never see what one day might be lost. It was breathtaking—like a scene out of a movie—and it only happened because I didn't allow my feet to take me back to the hotel. I just allowed myself to be led by the adventure.

RULE #4: TRY NEW THINGS

Sharing masgouf with Abu Haidar and his tribe in the marshlands near Chibayish was an unforgettable experience. Though the raw horsemeat outside of Yakutsk may not have been my favorite food, I enjoyed the chapatti and goat of Yemen; the hummus, falafel, kibbeh, and shawarma of Syria; the Nigerian fufu; and the unique foods of India, Japan, and so many other countries and regions around the world.

Sometimes it's scary or uncomfortable to try new foods, especially when it's something you've never seen or heard of before. But food is the main connector of the world, and sharing a meal with someone in a foreign country is perhaps the best way to travel. Food is the medium in which we create lifelong memories—connecting with other people and cultures. I don't take foodborne illnesses lightly, but having been hit with the stomach bug a few times, and in a few different countries, sometimes a rough night on the toilet is still worth the experience of connection, culture, and creating memories that will last a lifetime.

Obviously, you want to be careful and decide how risky you want to be with your culinary delights, but as I have discovered, we all have the same digestive systems, and usually if another culture can safely eat a food, so can you.

RULE #5: MEET NEW PEOPLE

By this point, I'm going to guess you will never travel again without making local friends! Revisit chapter six if you'd like a refresher on how to connect with locals before and during your travels.

In the Dutch-speaking country of Suriname, located in South America, I was staying at a nondescript hotel in the capital of Paramaribo. The hotel concierge told me about a local man named Steve, who tracks down anacondas in the Amazon. He asked me if I wanted to meet him, and I said absolutely. Well, that little conversation with the concierge turned into a four-day excursion with Steve and Deanna. We went on the back of his truck, through the dense jungles, and down to the southern part of the country. We slept in little tents and had the most amazing time tracking anacondas. And you know what? We didn't find a single one, but it didn't matter. Just by meeting Steve, we were taking on an adventure we never would have had, seeing parts of the world that most people never get to see. And we were reminded that life's best moments are always waiting to happen.

Don't forget about meeting other travelers as well. Many of the stories in this book are from meeting local people in the places I've visited, but some of my best friends have been made on the road. And it's always fun to meet other travelers because you have something in common: an interest to travel to that specific destination! I met one of my best friends, Dan, on a plane to Nauru (the world's least visited country with about two hundred visitors a year). We ended up staying at the same hotel, bonding over being Jewish travelers, and our love for different cultures.

Dan is from Melbourne, Australia, and over the years, we have met in Hong Kong, Somalia, Iran, and the Philippines. Though the places, food, and culture can be spectacular, the spontaneity of meeting and making new friends and experiences is what makes every challenge of travel worth it!

📍 Bangkok, Thailand

CHAPTER 10

How to Handle Crazy Shit
(And There Will Be Crazy Shit)

Fact: Getting trapped in America during a global pandemic was the worst part about my travels in the last ten years. In late February 2020, Deanna and I went to the Dominican Republic and Panama (two of my final eight countries). As soon as we returned to the US, we found out that everything was shutting down. I'll never forget when, on March 11, I was watching an NBA game on TV and in the middle of the game, they cancelled the rest of the season. Being stuck in the US was brutal—especially because I had just six countries left to complete my goal. In other words, I visited 99 percent of the world's countries, and then the world shut down.

We stayed at my parents' house in Arizona for three months before relocating to an Airbnb in Los Angeles. And LA was even more of a disaster.

I remember walking on the sidewalk in LA in the heart of the pandemic, and people wouldn't walk within a ten-foot radius of me or anyone else who walked by. All of the public beaches and parks were closed, and all restaurants were take-out only. It was a wild experience.

After years of hopping on planes and traveling the world, I now couldn't go anywhere at all. And though everyone experienced the same thing, the immediate stop was jarring, on my schedule, my business, my whole life. For the first time in years, I had no other choice but to sit there and do nothing. It was really the first time in my life that I was told, "No, you cannot travel, you're blocked."

Instead, I began to reflect on the last eight years of travel—of all of these stories, the people I had met, the friends I made, the countries I had been to, and the ones I had yet to visit.

In May 2020, I managed to slowly get back on the road again. There were only four countries open at the time—Mexico, Tanzania, Turkey, and Egypt. So I went to Mexico, for five weeks. And it was a fantastic trip. And it was the first time that I had explored inland, as opposed to keeping to the coastal beach towns, and Mexico quickly jumped in the rankings as one of my favorite countries. There is so much to offer there in terms of culture, and the food is fantastic!

After Mexico, I proceeded to Turkey, Egypt, Iraq, Afghanistan, and Tanzania over the next six months. So much was still shut down, and in the countries where there was already little Western presence, it felt like I was the only traveler in the world. Meanwhile, I tried to figure out how I was going to finish my last six countries to complete my journey to all 197: Ghana, Ecuador, Venezuela, Palau, Jamaica, and Saudi Arabia.

My business took a massive hit because nobody was really interested in traveling. It was very tough to push through those months, not to mention trying to film stories about humanity when everyone was wearing masks and you couldn't see their smiles! Thankfully, our planet was able to persevere and get through the worst parts of the pandemic, and as I write this, we are just about back to normal. After Japan reopened, I was one of the first tourists back in 2.5 years, and though everyone was still masked up, everything was open!

Hopefully, we never have to deal with a global pandemic again in our lifetimes, but we know that the unexpected can always happen. So let's get some ground rules for handling crazy shit when shit hits the fan—because you and I both know that there will be situations that come up.

KNOW HOW TO STAY CALM (NO MATTER WHAT)

As I touched on in previous chapters, staying calm is really important. If there's an attack or kidnapping or something of that nature, you must stay calm—no matter what crisis you're facing.

Earlier in this book, I briefly mentioned getting to meet members of a Pygmy tribe. I flew into Bangui, which is the capital city of the Central African Republic, where I was meeting my local friend David. He was a friend of a friend, a college student, and an all-around great guy. David and I decided to drive seven hours, picking up a local translator along the way, to meet a Pygmy tribe. Their lives are so interesting to me because they live in complete isolation in the rainforest, and they rely on what the land provides for food, water, and shelter. But to get there, we had to drive seven hours in a small truck with five other people, across Gabon, the Democratic Republic of the Congo (DRC), Burundi, Uganda, and Central African Republic. There were so many checkpoints along the way—and I didn't know if this military was made up of rebels or the actual police.

During these tense moments, I had to stay calm. I didn't know if I was going to get kidnapped, scammed, or both. I didn't know anything other than I had a story I wanted to tell, and sometimes there's risk involved in telling a great story.

> **In staying calm, we get to remain present—for both the great moments and the hard ones; deepening our understanding of the places we visit and the joys and challenges of their cultures.**

When local officials see a foreigner, or anyone with white skin who doesn't have a UN identification (there are hundreds working in the Central African Republic), then a lot of eyebrows get raised. And unfortunately, in that part of the world, bribery is rampant. Our driver was giving bribes to the police every time we were stopped, which was probably twenty times on this drive. They would hold us and make up a story like "your back light is out" and they'd wait for us to pay.

What was supposed to be a seven-hour drive ended up taking eleven hours, but in the end, we made it. We stayed calm and quiet no matter how long the police made us wait—or how many times we had to bribe them to get through. And it was so worth it! I was able to spend more than twenty-four hours with the Pygmy tribe, and they welcomed me with open arms and smiles. They told me that they've never received a foreign visitor nor seen a white person in their entire lives. We sat around the fire, drank palm wine (which David had bought from local villages on the trek over), and bonded just through emotion and gestures. It was an experience that I'll never forget!

KNOW THE LOCAL LAWS

You have to know the basics of the local laws in the country that you are visiting. It's not necessary to study them before going, but having general awareness of what you legally can and can't do is important for your safety. Remember: you are a visitor in another country with another government and a set of laws that is different than those where you come from.

I was traveling on a two-week road trip in West Africa with my Spanish friend, Alvaro. We were crossing the land border from Liberia to Sierra Leone. We had no issues with the Liberian officials; however, when we got to Sierra Leone, things changed.

Whenever you're in doubt, trust your instincts. And the more you travel, the stronger your instincts will become.

"Excuse me, sir, I am going to need you to come this way," one of the immigrations officials announced after checking our paperwork at customs. Any time you do not immediately get a stamp on your papers and get waved through is cause for concern, but also, all the more reason to stay calm. The officials took us into a back room that looked like an elementary school classroom, ordering us to sit down. Both officials were forty-something with bald heads, and they did not look happy. I noticed all of these notices on the wall of vaccines that were mandatory to enter Sierra Leone.

They pointed to the wall and said, "You need a cholera vaccine and yellow fever vaccine to enter our country."

We showed them our yellow fever vaccine paperwork—which is needed to enter most countries in Sub-Saharan Africa and told them that we don't need the cholera one because it's not mandatory. As I've mentioned, it's important to know what vaccines are required where, not only to get into each country, but also to be informed should you find yourself in any weird situations like this one. The customs officials demanded a $500 payment from each of us. When we refused, one of the men opened up a drawer and pulled out a loaded syringe. Flicking the point of the needle, he said, "Okay then, we will give you the cholera vaccine right now. Give me your left arm."

We didn't know what was in the vaccine, but we did know that we were being blackmailed to refuse it. I remained calm on the outside though I was furious on the inside, but Alvaro erupted. We knew that we were getting scammed. After twenty minutes of debating, we negotiated the bribe down to $150 each and paid.

It's so important to know the local laws, rules, and customs so you can be prepared for any unexpected situations like what happened to me in Sierra Leone. And remember that having extra US cash can sometimes bail you out of trouble. Then, you just take deep breath, and move on.

Five Types of Crazy Shit and What to Do When They Happen

1. Aggressive taxi drivers—When I was in Istanbul, the guy who drove me from the airport to the hotel must have dodged four legitimate accidents while driving 90 mph down the freeway. Be wary of unmarked taxis. When you can, try to take public transportation or an Uber (which at least offers you more safety since the app tracks you). Always try to travel the way the locals do, because they often know the safest and quickest ways across their city.

2. Drunk people—When I was in Bogotá, Colombia, with Deanna, we were both stalked by a drunk man who was holding a bottle of rum. As we walked across the street, he would walk across the street and stare at us. I quickly Googled the nearest police station and we fast walked there to find safety. Though it's fun to go out and party, try to stay away from any large drunken groups or anyone who is acting erratic. As a foreigner, you can easily become a target. That's why it's best to go out with people from the area, because they can help guide you out of a dangerous situation—and will usually help to navigate any tricky interactions.

3. Fights—When I was in Bangkok, I walked down the backpackers' street called Khaosan Road and I popped into a bar that was packed with foreigners. Sure enough, the

moment I stepped into the bar area, two Brits had their shirts off and were fistfighting while others were watching. As with the drunk people mentioned above, if you see large groups or even just two people getting into a physical fight, it's best to stay away and get away, if you can. You never know how local authorities might respond to a situation, and you don't want to be caught up in something even more violent or dangerous. Though you might be more aggressive or even just curious in your own country, remember you don't always know the rules or customs when things get heated.

4. Police officers—When I was in Belarus, I was stopped on the street by a police officer for simply carrying my DSLR camera over my shoulder. I had to explain to him that I was only capturing photos and videos for personal use, not professional use (which was a lie), and after a very awkward five-minute conversation, he let me go. The truth is, police, even in our own country, can be amazingly helpful or they can be dangerous. You need to know when and how to approach them, and, if you need help, whether or not the police in that area are the best people to go to. If I've said it once, I'll say it a million times: knowing local people can help you to navigate the customs and concerns around local authorities. And don't get me wrong, there are a lot of wonderful police out there, but there are also some who abuse their power—and you need to be cautious how you interact with them.

5. Grandmas (you never know where they will steer you!)— As much as we love the nonnas, nanas, and yiayias of the world, be careful asking them for directions, driving up on

their properties, or disrespecting them in any way. Grand-
mothers rule the world, and they can send you down a
number of wrong streets with their directions! And if you
ever doubt this, try asking an old Italian lady for directions.
Grandmas can be ruthless, and many hold older ideas on
visitors and foreigners based on the histories they have
lived through.

KNOW WHEN TO LIE

Lower-risk travelers probably won't run into situations when you have to
lie, but if you're going on big adventures, sometimes big trouble is hard to
avoid. And though I don't advocate lying, it might the only way out of a
situation, or in the case of my visit to Libya, the only way into one.

Libya's history goes way back thousands of years to ancient civiliza-
tions. The Berbers (these days more commonly known as the Amazigh or
Imazighen) are the main ethnic group of North Africa, and they settled
in this hot and dry land located in the world's largest desert—the Sahara.
Many people don't know that in more modern times, Libya was colonized
by Italy. Yes—Italy! There were very few Italian colonies, but Libya was one
of them. To this day, there remains a lot of Italian influence in the cafés, the
architecture, the language, the food, and of course, the gelato. Libyans are
multilingual, multiethnic, and a multireligious people. Many of them can
speak Arabic, Italian, and English. It's truly a fascinating place.

In terms of amazing sites and world wonders, Libya is as impressive as
they come. There's a settlement in the north called Leptis Magna. Leptis
Magna was a beautiful ancient Roman city with two-thousand-plus-year-
old amphitheaters, houses, bathhouses, and hieroglyphics that's surrounded
by mountains in all directions. At its peak, it held over 200,000 residents,

which, in my opinion, is the most preserved Roman ruin in the world. Better than anything in Italy, Greece, Turkey, Lebanon, or Israel.

When I visited Leptis Magna, it was so special because there were no other tourists. It was just me and my local friend/tour guide named Ibrahim. It's also right on the ocean, so you get the most stunning views and breeze. I mean, if this site was anywhere else in the world, like France, then it would get ten million visitors a year. But this is Libya, with nobody else around.

It was an experience like no other. And I almost didn't make it there. Because Libya's visa is one of the world's hardest to get, for any nationality.

And sometimes, it's okay to lie—in the case of Libya, it was the only way to get in. The Libyan government does not issue tourist visas (for political reasons). They only issue business visas. And in order to get a business visa, you need to go in person to either the Libyan embassy in Washington, DC, or to the one in Rome.

At the time, I was traveling in the Middle East. I was in Syria, Afghanistan, Iraq, Lebanon, and Jordan.

When it came to Libya, my local guide/fixer, Ibrahim, told me, "You need to go to Rome to get the visa." So, I went to Rome.

The reason why it's so complicated to travel to Libya is because of their ongoing civil war, which has been exacerbated by a nasty political crisis. More than a decade ago, the former leader Muammar al-Qaddafi was executed, and since then, Libya has struggled to end its violent conflict, and the borders have seen nothing but an increase of trafficking and smuggling of illegal things such as drugs and weapons. In short, it's a mess.

But I was determined to get there, no matter what it cost.

So, I spent an obnoxious amount of money on a plane ticket, a hotel, and food for a week in Rome. Though it was only supposed to be two days because they told me I could expedite the visa! Turns out that was also a lie. I had to keep extending my hotel every night because I wasn't sure which day I would get the visa. It ended up coming at the last minute before my trip. I literally went to the Libyan embassy to pick up my passport and then went straight to the airport to fly to Tunisia (because Tunisia had the only flight to Tripoli, Libya's capital).

However, in order to get my visa, I had to lie and say that I was an oil consultant, because it's the only way I was allowed in. I even dressed in disguise—with nice clothes and a briefcase (that I picked up in Syria a few weeks before). When I got to immigration in Tripoli, they were skeptical. They asked me: "What company do you work for?"

I froze. Then I said, "Oh, I'm self-employed."

And they replied, "Okay, come to the back room."

I was sweating bullets.

They investigated me. I was asked literally every question for thirty minutes, and I was by myself. Meanwhile, I had my Sony camera in my bag, which is a *big* no-no—had they seen it, I would be captured and maybe taken to jail and accused of being an undercover spy.

They do not want journalists to document anything because of the ongoing civil war. About thirty minutes after being interrogated in that small room with no windows, one of the scariest moments of my life happened. As I was answering their questions in the back room, I suddenly heard a lot of gunshots. POP POP POP. I freaked out, jumped out of the chair, grabbed my briefcase, and bolted for the door.

They told me that it was fireworks (and clearly I was the only tourist around). That moment broke the ice—I finally saw some smiles from the police officers—and probably convinced them that I wasn't a spy because what kind of spy would lose their cool like that? And yes, even though you're not supposed to lose your cool, sometimes we all lose our cool.

They ended up letting me through because I gave them the number of my driver, and he explained to them that I was, in fact, an oil consultant on a business trip to Libya. Everything was a lie. But I don't feel guilty because

📍 **Four Corners, USA** | I've made my name from international travel, but I love getting around to cool places here in the United States, too—like the Four Corners Monument, where the states of Arizona, New Mexico, Colorado, and Utah all meet.

📍 **Leptis Magna, Libya** | Can you believe that the most preserved Roman ruins that I've ever seen are in Libya? Despite being in the country during a civil war (and falling asleep to my bed shaking from nearby bombs), this is one of the most stunning sites I've ever seen. And I had it all to myself!

Seoul, South Korea | At Bukchon Hanok Village, an area of Seoul that has many restored traditional Korean houses, called *hanok*.

Siquijor, Philippines | Deanna's home country of the Philippines is one of the most beautiful places in the world. Here I am enjoying the view.

📍 **Seoul, South Korea** | On a popular shopping street called Myeongdong. It's famous for beauty products and fashion, but if you're not into shopping you can also catch a traditional performance at one of its many theaters.

📍 **Solomon Islands** | Underwater diving with sharks. I've been on more than thirty dives around the world from Fiji to Honduras to Mauritius!

📍 **Boom, Belgium** | The Tomorrowland Music Festival is a huge EDM festival. Every year there's a different theme and a different incredible design for the main stage. (top left)

📍 **El Salvador** | Volcano hopping. El Salvador has twenty volcanoes. Most have been dormant for a long time, though San Miguel, in eastern El Salvador, erupted in 2023. (bottom left)

📍 **Kabul, Afghanistan** | Horse riding trips can be a great way to see remote parts of many countries you visit. (top right)

📍 **Bohol, Philippines** | The Chocolate Hills are an incredible geographical formation. There are more than a thousand of these hills spread over an area of 50 square kilometers. The grass that covers the hills turns brown in the dry season, and that's where they got their name.

📍 **Stuttgart, Germany** | The Cannstatter Volksfest (known to visitors as the Stuttgart Beer Fest) is Europe's second-largest beer festival, behind Oktoberfest in Munich. Deanna and I definitely wanted to dress the part.

◆ Koh Samui, Thailand | Throwback to my early days of backpacking, standing on a dock in Koh Samui.

◆ Kyiv, Ukraine | On top of what's now called the Mother Ukraine Monument. In 2023, Ukraine removed the Soviet hammer and sickle from her shield (where I am in this photo) and replaced it with the trident symbol.

📍 Uyuni, Bolivia | The salt flats in southern Bolivia are the largest salt flats on Earth, extending more than 4,000 square miles. This picture captures just a small piece of their extreme beauty.

📍 Page, Arizona, USA | There's extreme beauty to be found in the US, too. Here's Horseshoe Bend—sometimes called the "east rim of the Grand Canyon"—in my home state of Arizona.

that's the only way I could get inside. I wasn't able to use my camera much because it was forbidden—so I used my phone to document the trip.

Was it worth it? Yes, absolutely. Would I do it again? In a heartbeat.

And I don't feel like it was unethical. I felt like it was the right thing to do because I was now able to see and share stories from Libya, which was amazing. But the whole time, I still had to keep a low profile.

> **Sometimes adventure requires that we take risks—going past our comfort zones to discover what is out there.**

Many Libyans speak Italian and drive Italian cars. It was a cool, interesting place. But yeah, all in all, it's the most expensive trip I've taken. If I factor in the costs of being in Rome, the hotel renewals, the visa cost, the package tour, etc., we are looking at $4,500 for a three-day trip. That is absurd, but all worth it in the end! That is the price that you have to pay to get into Libya—and that's why it's important to know how to bullshit your way through certain situations.

If Yemen is the world's most dangerous country, then Libya is number two. There is an ongoing civil war, and I actually fell asleep each night to the sound of bombs rumbling my bed frame. The bombs were just ten miles away from me. It was bizarre. But just as I experienced when the world shut down in 2020, being prepared for the unexpected is what makes travel—and living—into an adventure.

No matter what life throws at you, you have to adjust and make the best of it. Because, believe me, shit happens all the time, and things don't always go your way. You might get terribly sick in a foreign country, your taxi driver might get in a car crash (or worse, a bus crash like I had in India), you might get rained out on your only two days on a tropical island. At the end of the day, it is up to you make the most of any given situation. As long as you keep pushing yourself outside your comfort zone and believing in yourself, you can always learn to manage the unexpected—and usually make something amazing out of it! When looking back on some of my best trips and travel moments, there is always some crazy shit that was involved that didn't go according to plan. And that was the juiciest part!

Like during lockdown. During my months at home, I decided to see America instead, taking road trips around our country, and at a time when it felt like we were so isolated and disconnected, I met people all over America. And I didn't even need to fly to get into the country. Because as much as I wanted to leave, I was also home.

📍 Coron, Philippines

CHAPTER 11

Have Fun!

I have to acknowledge that a lot of this book has talked about stressful moments, planning for the worst, and what to do if you get stuck in unfortunate situations. But what about taking it easy? After all, that's really the goal of traveling—to escape from your everyday reality and enjoy yourself. To put your job on hold, forget about the stresses in your daily life, and be present in the moment.

When you close your eyes and think about travel, the most obvious things that come to mind are positive moments—whether it's the most pristine beach you've seen or the best meal of your life or the most fascinating landmarks on Earth. And that's a good thing! Sometimes, we need to put up with some crap (i.e., flight delays, getting sick, etc.) before the best moments come out—and so in this chapter, I want to talk about how to make the most of the good stuff!

SLOW IT DOWN

Stop moving so fast. Stop running from point A to point B. Stop trying to get wherever you think you need to be. Because the best part of travel happens when you least expect it. Hit the brakes, listen, and realize that you're always going to get to wherever you need to be. Things always have a funny way of working themselves out in the end.

When you slow down, you have more time to open up your eyes and ears and learn something new. You'll feel more present and deeply immersed in the place, culture, and people you're talking to. You'll actually get to know the area you're visiting, rather than just seeing it.

Back in 2015, I was backpacking around Europe. These were some of my early days of travel, and I visited twenty countries in two months. That's an average of one country every three days. Even though most European countries are smaller than US states, I didn't have any time to really take things in. I was always on the go—moving to the next place, slamming down a meal, driving fast to get to the next city. Looking back now, thankfully, I've been able to revisit all of these countries, but I do regret how fast I moved on that journey because I didn't get to soak it in and enjoy the moment. If I were to redo that trip, I would spend more time sitting in coffee shops, walking through the cities, and just being in the cultures I was having the chance to explore.

One of my favorite travel moments last year was being in Amsterdam in Vondelpark—one of the most beautiful parks in the world. I spent every hour of daylight—from 8 AM to 10 PM (the farther north you go, the later the sun sets in the summer!)—just sitting on a bench and walking slowly around the park. I felt recharged. My mental health was in a great state for the rest of the trip. Everything, all of a sudden, made sense.

And look, we all need days off. It's important to also slow down every now and then—whether sitting in a park or visiting a library or spending the day in a hotel bed.

Sometimes, we can get so caught up in the next thing we have to do or see that we forget that resting is part of the adventure too.

And it's important to take that space to help you refresh and get the energy to start your next adventure.

TAKE IT EASY

Jamaica was my second to last country (196/197), and oh boy, was it a blast!

Jamaica is so good on so many levels, and I'm very happy that I saved it for the end of my quest. Sometimes it is important to "do as the Romans do." So even though I'm not much of a marijuana smoker, I did try it while I was in Jamaica, and it was wonderful. But more than just trying it, I learned all about it—which led me to a massive field of marijuana in the countryside. People in Jamaica smoke a lot of weed, and they love living the high life.

In Jamaica, it's legal to grow and harvest, and it's baked into their culture. You may already know about the weed culture of Jamaica from listening to Bob Marley; he was actually the one who pioneered the movement for open marijuana laws in the country—or, as they call it, "ganja." The culture is so inviting, with their Rastafarian beliefs (which is both a religion and a lifestyle), as well as their reggae music that just makes you feel good.

While in Jamaica, I met up with a local friend named Matt, who is a fellow content creator, and he took me under his wing for twelve days. The two of us traveled all around the country, starting in the hectic capital city of Kingston, then working up toward Montego Bay, where the beaches are fantastic. Along the way, we stopped at so many jerk chicken stalls (the best!) and got lost in the jungle.

My favorite part of Jamaica was visiting a mountain range where we had to hike up thousands of stairs. All of a sudden, we arrived at this little Rastafarian village with around thirty families living there. I stumbled upon another marijuana farm and then a Rastafarian temple where the people introduced me to their religion and way of life, which is so peaceful! I was surprised to see how spiritual they are, repeating the words "to the holy testament," and it was also interesting to see how they idolize Israel and wear the Star of David symbol around their necks. The friendly guys there gave me a walking tour of their neighborhood, which is situated on an uphill slant on the top of a mountain.

"Hey brotha, where you come from?" asked one Rasta guy with dreadlocks down to the floor.

"I'm from Arizona—ever heard of it?"

"Oh yeah, oh yeah. We love America because you guys appreciate our lives and our music." He nodded before replying with Jamaica's version of "Aloha": "One love."

On the way up, we walked through wheat farms and vegetable farms, and they told me about their diet—which is called "Ital." Ital food is fully vegan and natural, free from additives, chemicals, and most meats. They even offered to cook up a meal overlooking the stunning viewpoint, and after 195 countries—and one global pandemic—it felt like the perfect moment to celebrate that I was almost there.

> **We need to also make time to slow down and to have fun on our travels—there is more to a place than just sights to see and stories to tell. And the more we connect with the fun of a locale, the more we come to know it.**

Jamaica is one of the best places in the world to completely unplug, relax, and take it slow. Nobody is in a hurry there! And as far as I'm concerned, there is no better place in the Caribbean than Jamaica—it's one of the only locations in the world where everything you've heard about it is true!

In case you were wondering, two other countries in the Caribbean that offer as much in terms of culture, beauty, and positive vibes are Cuba and the Dominican Republic. Both are absolutely incredible, and I will keep returning to them time and time again.

DIVE IN!

Palau is a tiny island in the South Pacific, not far away from the Philippines, but with fewer than 18,000 residents. To put that population into perspective, more people fit in Madison Square Garden than live in Palau. Palau was my fourth to last country, and I went in July 2021—right when the country opened after being shut down for over a year. I was so excited to be on the very first passenger plane back to this land they call paradise!

Palau is another island nation, but it is in no way similar to Jamaica. It is filled with natural wonders that don't exist anywhere else and the most pristine crystal-clear ocean that you could possibly imagine. It's like looking through glass to see an abundance of sea life. And Palau takes great measures to preserve their nature by making you sign a declaration, the "Palau Pledge," on your passport upon arrival. They do this to make sure that visitors act in an ecologically and culturally responsible way on the island, for the sake of Palau's children and future generations. The country was the first (and is still the only) nation on Earth to change its immigration laws for the cause of environmental protection.

I had two full weeks in Palau, which is about a week and a half longer than anyone else I've ever met who's been there. The main island is so small that you can cover everything in just a few hours, and the outer islands are absolutely worth a visit as well. I was lucky enough to meet the president, Mr. Surangel Whipps, Jr., and spent a lot of time with him and his brother (who hosted me at his house). When I say the word "president," it sounds so official and formal, but in fact, he's just a normal guy, and his role is more of a community leader (like a pastor of a church), given that the country is so small.

If there's any one activity or sport that I recommend you take part in when traveling, it is scuba diving. I got PADI (Professional Association of Diving Instructors) certified in Coron, Philippines, in 2015, and since then, I've been on more than thirty dives around the world from Fiji to Honduras to Mauritius. The cost for getting your PADI certification varies from $300–$800, depending on the country that you are in. In the Philippines, I paid $300.

I recognize it might not be in everyone's budget, but in other countries, it can certainly be way less expensive than getting your certification in the US or other Western countries.

And depending on what country you're in, what's in the sea can be just as, if not more, incredible than what you might find on land. The diving in Palau is the world's best. And these words are not mine—they are from some of the world's most experienced divers. As soon as you enter that warm water, you will be blown away by the diverse life that lives below the surface. There are dozens of shipwrecks from WWII that you can roam around, which have become playgrounds for manatees, sharks, and stingrays.

> **As much as there might be to see on land, there is nothing like exploring the magic and mystery found in our world's oceans, seas, rivers, lakes, and bayous.**

As you dive under the water, the current is so strong that you must stay near the side of the coral wall. Once you get about one hundred feet below the surface, they strap you into the coral with a hook, and you open up your arms like Superman and float while you're looking at a variety of sharks pass two feet in front of you. It's pure magic! Each dive ranges from $50–$200 USD.

Also, there's Jellyfish Lake, which is a bizarre natural phenomenon and a UNESCO World Heritage Site. The lake is just a few meters away from the open sea, separated by a row of limestone cliffs, but inside of the lake are tens of millions of stingless jellyfish! They evolved without their stingers because there are no predators in the lake. It's so eerie to swim through jellyfish—literally touching them as you go—and not have to worry about them stinging you!

But if being underwater is not your thing, Palau still has a lot to offer. You can go parasailing, fishing, speedboat racing, or just relax at one of the many insanely beautiful beaches.

Palau is a dream, and I highly invite you to add it to your bucket list for an experience you'll never forget! Treating yourself to a trip like Palau or Jamaica is some of the best kind of fun that you can have on this planet. But the word "fun" is subjective, right? What is fun to me might not be fun to you. Fun experiences come in many shapes, forms, and sizes.

GO PARTY

To some of you reading this, having fun means nightlife—going to bars, clubs, and festivals, and having some drinks while dancing to music and meeting strangers. And that WAS fun for me from ages eighteen through twenty-four! As I mentioned, my very first travel blog when I moved to South Korea to teach English in 2013 was called *The Hungry Partier*. On that website, I would write about food and nightlife experiences around the world. And that's kind of what got me plugged into the world of content creation.

Obviously, being the "Hungry Partier" wasn't all I wanted to do. As much as I love food and drinking, I really loved meeting and connecting with people and sharing their stories, so I slowly evolved my brand into just my name, Drew Binsky.

But I still like nightlife. I still like partying and meeting people and having fun. And you know, sometimes going out at night can show you a lot about a place! And remember that dancing is an international language. Most people love to dance and have fun. Nightlife is also a chance for people to flirt and get to know each other. I met my now wife while traveling—as you know—and I have learned of so many romantic travel connections. Going out and meeting new people is a huge part of traveling anywhere.

> **Nightlife is where you can really get to know people—having fun, making memories, and enjoying some of the most shared human activities: dancing, drinking, and flirting!**

But after partying in (literally) 150 cities and countries around the world, the one that surprised me the most was Lagos, Nigeria.

There's a lot happening on the streets of Lagos—and sometimes the number of honking horns you'll hear can be quite overwhelming. There's one street in Lagos, near a beach, which every night turns into a festival with lights, street food BBQ, beach parties, concerts, and bars that are serving beer, cocktails, and palm wine—a local favorite. Nigerians are some of the most outgoing folks in Africa. Nigerians speak English as a first language, so if you go to Nigeria, you'll be able to understand everything around you! While wandering around the busiest street market in Lagos, I bumped into a nineteen-year-old street magician performing on the street.

"What's going on, man?" I asked him.

He introduced himself. "Hey, bro, my name is Babs Cardini. I perform on the streets for the people."

And before I knew it, Babs was showing me his act as he approached a group of ten construction workers wearing hard hats; he told one of them to pick a card and sign it and not to show him.

Babs shuffled the deck for a while and eventually told the worker to check his back pocket, where he pulled out the card. Everyone freaked out, running around the streets screaming. It really was a pleasure to witness! I have a feeling that he will be on the *Today Show* someday; this kid has got some real potential.

In a way, the country is comparable to Hollywood, as much of Africa's best music, movies, and arts come out of Nigeria.

Much of the music is centered around Afrobeat, a genre that was originated in Nigeria by an artist named Fela back in the 1990s. Bob Marley is to reggae what Fela is to Afrobeat. I went to a venue called "Fela's Shrine," which is the venue where he used to perform to massive crowds. This place is electric inside, full of energy, palm wine, memorabilia of Fela, marijuana stands, and about 1,500 people packed tightly together and enjoying the night. Believe me, I've experienced some pretty wild nightlife scenes across Africa—like raving at a Kentucky Fried Chicken in Luanda, Angola (where KFC would hire DJs to come and they would eat chicken, drink beer, and dance), or all-night drinking at a brewery in Windhoek, Namibia—but what I experienced in Lagos was unparalleled to anywhere else on the continent.

The Five Best Places to Party

Other notable places around the world with a very fun nightlife scene are listed below. Keep in mind that you don't have to drink to have a good time!

1. Dubai, United Arab Emirates—Even though UAE is technically a "dry" country, meaning you can't buy booze from any stores, there are plenty of bars and clubs that are attached to international hotel chains. Some places in Dubai put Vegas to shame—there is a rooftop infinity pool and bar on the seventieth floor of a building that simply is unmatched by anything anywhere else in the world.

2. Rio de Janeiro, Brazil—Never have I ever seen more beautiful people coming together in one place at one time than in Rio. Copacabana Beach is where it's at—friendly people walking around enjoying life and having a great time. And don't forget to eat as much acai as humanly possible.

3. Seoul, South Korea—They say that NYC is the city that never sleeps, but Manhattan has nothing on Seoul. South Korea's capital city is very much a 24-7 society in terms of restaurants, convenience stores, bars, and clubs. It's not unusual to walk out of a club at 7 AM and stumble into a Korean BBQ restaurant. It's as good as it gets!

4. Budapest, Hungary—Hungarians in Budapest invented "ruin pubs," which are basically underground bunkers that were used as shelters during WWII, and they've converted them into the most incredible bars in Europe. There are about five ruin pubs in Budapest, each with differently themed rooms that range from a 1960s chemistry lab to living in the future like *The Matrix*.

5. Bangkok, Thailand—It's hard to not like Thailand's capital city. And with thirty million visitors a year, I'm clearly not the only one who thinks so! Bangkok has a lot to offer, from its party boats over the river, to the backpackers' district called Khaosan Road, to more upscale places where you need to dress to impress.

Learning and discovering and tasting and feeling are all part of the journey, and at the end of the day, traveling the world should always be FUN. So as much as my travels have been about learning and sharing (and I hope you do both of those too), make having fun your number one priority.

During the times you are feeling stressed, try to close your eyes, take three deep breaths, and remember the reason you are traveling in the first place—and that might be a very different reason for all of us.

And remember, "having fun" doesn't have to mean the same to you as it does to someone else. What are your passions? Whatever things you enjoy in your everyday life at home, you can elevate them in your journeys! Are you a golfer? Then add golf to your itineraries! Are you a scuba diver? You better get after the islands of the world! Are you an avid break-dancer? There are break-dancing communities in every city in the world, waiting for you to arrive. Maybe you are a cocktail connoisseur and want to visit all of the top one hundred–ranked bars around the world. Or perhaps you are into ghosts, and you want to visit the most haunted places on the planet.

Or better yet, use traveling as the gateway to start a new hobby! Try learning how to cook pad thai in Bangkok, how to tango in Argentina, or how to do Tae Kwon Do in South Korea—I've brought home so many hobbies and new interests because I tried them out in the places where they originated. Travel provides endless opportunities to have fun and enjoy yourself, so you can collect memories and share them with the people you love—or even with the wider world.

Share the Journey

Sharing my journey with my friends, family, and followers on social media has been an enriching and powerful experience. Never before have we been able to so easily share our adventures in real time, and I have proudly taken advantage of this generation on the internet. By being a travel vlogger, I am able to share stories from the hidden sides

📍 Paris, France

PART FOUR

of our world and hopefully educate and inspire others to follow me there. I hope that my stories make an impact on how we view other people and cultures, and ultimately, help spread the message that "We Are All the Same."

Because we are.

How to Say "Goodbye" Around the World

Language | Most common way to say hello | *Pronunciation*

Amharic | Bayi (ባይ) | *Bai*

Arabic | Mae alsalama (مع السلامة) | *May ahsahlahmah*

Burmese | Swarrtotmaal (သွားတော့မယ်) | *Swar-toh-meal*

English | See you soon | *See-yoo-soon*

Farsi | Khoda hafis (خداحافظ) | *Koo-dah ha-fiz*

Filipino | Paalam | *Pah-lahm*

French | Au revoir | *Oh-VWAHR*

Hebrew | Shalom (הֱיה שלום) | *Shah-lohm*

Indonesian | Selamat tinggal | *Sell-ah-maht teen-gahl*

Korean | Annyeong (안녕) | *AN-nyeong*

Kurdish | Bi xatirê te | *By scat-er teh*

Pashto | Da khoday pa amaan (د خدای په امان) | *Dah khod-ay pah ah-mahn*

Portuguese | Adeus | *Ah-deh-ooSH*

Russian | Do svidaniya (до свидания) | *Do-sve-DAN-ya*

Samoan | Tōfā | *Toe-fah*

Spanish | Adios | *Ah-dee-ows*

Swahili | Kwaheri | *Kwaheri*

Turkish | Güle güle | *Gooleh gooleh*

Ukrainian | Do pobachennya (до побачення) | *Doh-poh-ba-CHAN-ya*

Urdu | Khuda hafiz (خدا حافظ) | *Koo-dah ha-fiz*

Hanoi, Vietnam

CHAPTER 12

How to Share Your Journey

O nce, when I was traveling in Karachi, Pakistan, a philosopher that I met told me, "You are a present-day prophet."

I almost started to laugh. Me? A prophet?? But then he explained, "Prophets are just messengers . . . What you're doing in your videos is a modern form of communication, with similar messages about humanity that prophets once shared."

And I want to continue being a messenger.

To have more than eight billion views on my videos across platforms is a blessing. It's been such an amazing opportunity so far, and the best part is that I feel like I'm just getting started. There is a lot more to do and accomplish as I work to build and grow this community of travelers around the world. It takes a hell of a lot of work, managing my growing team of twenty-two people (from editors to cinematographers to graphic designers to production managers), and then chasing the best stories around the world.

Granted, not everyone sees the same potential in life as a YouTuber. I am often asked, "Are you really enjoying your trips? When you go places for three days, and you're in front of the camera the whole time, is it fun?"

My answer is, "YES!"

The truth is, I get more satisfaction from being able to document and share my adventures with tens of millions of people every month than I do from living the experiences myself. And my videos live forever. When I'm seventy-five years old, I'll still be able to watch them! And yes, I do have times where I put my camera down and enjoy and be present—I do find a lot of value in unplugging and reflecting. But I believe strongly in YouTube and social media as the future of how we learn about the world. It's so important for me to share my journeys and connect with people on these platforms. And not only did I write this book to inspire you to travel, but also to let you know that there are opportunities for you to do what I did—turn a passion into a career.

ANYONE CAN DO IT (AND I MEAN THAT: ANYONE!)

You—yes, you—can make a living purely off your interests. If my parents heard that, growing up in their generation, they wouldn't have believed it to be true. And still, when I meet anyone over the age of fifty and try to explain to them that this is what I do for a living, they just don't believe me.

For any amateurs out there who want to start making content for a living, if I can do it, you can do it, too! I'm just a regular guy who grew up in suburban Phoenix, Arizona. As soon as I graduated college, I did every-thing on my own; I figured everything out. I haven't taken any money from my parents. If you are reading this and you have the internet, which would be 99.99 percent of you, then you can do it too. Anyone with a phone can start making videos about their passions and put them online to monetize.

Now, before we go on, I will admit that I am lucky. The timing of me choosing to visit every country in the world and documenting it online certainly played to my advantage. I was born in 1991, right before the inter-net took off and changed the world forever. I got my first cell phone when I was in sixth grade, when smartphones had just become accessible. I got a MacBook Pro when I went to college—the 2012 version, which was the breakthrough edition that changed the way we are able to work from anywhere in the world. And I became a YouTuber in 2016, back when the word "YouTuber" didn't really exist yet; the platform of YouTube was around, but making a living from it wasn't really an option. And so, right when I started visiting every country and going to the world's faraway places, I was able to document my journeys and make money by putting them up online through ad revenue and brand sponsors.

The money was slow for the first few years, but then things really picked up, and now I have a team of twenty people working remotely (and representing nine countries). In short, I am running a production house, and it's really exciting and fun!

Looking back, I got very lucky with the timing, and I took advantage of it. Had I been born five years earlier, I would have missed having the option to do this for a living. Had I been born five years later, I could have certainly still done it, but with a much more competitive and saturated market of content creators. Being born in 1991 was just the sweet spot!

Still, I firmly believe that now is a great time to get started, and there's still a lot of room for passionate, creative people to find their audience online. Being a YouTuber, or content creator, is unique because there are so many different ways that you can do it. People have made entire careers out of things like mukbang (where they broadcast videos of themselves eating), tutorials, product reviews, and autonomous sensory meridian response (ASMR) videos, just to name a few. (Side note, if you don't know what ASMR is, then please stop what you're doing and type it on YouTube. Yes, there are people making millions of dollars a year off just doing strange sound effects into the camera.) There are thousands of tech-savvy folks who are making a living by reviewing every new phone and computer and gadget that comes out. And then all of a sudden, Samsung and Apple are sending them free stuff and paying them to review their products. That's pretty cool.

Now I will say that it does take a certain kind of person to be willing to be in front of the camera every day, as well as writing scripts, editing, uploading, and learning the YouTube game (for instance, it took me a while to learn that thumbnails are just as important as the video itself). You need to have that drive and that willingness to be in front of the lens. If videos aren't your thing, but you are still interested in getting into this crazy world of content creation, then you can become a blogger, which will require just as much dedication, but in the form of writing!

My Top Ten Tips for Becoming a Travel Vlogger

1. Post weekly. If you want people to stay interested, you need to be offering them consistent content.

2. Establish a brand that represents YOU. Share what matters most to you, and it will likely find an audience who cares about the same things.

3. Respond to comments and engage with your audience. You build online relationships just like any other relationship, by giving it time and attention.

4. Be consistent with storytelling. Find your voice and your message and then refine it as you go.

5. Find out how to stand out from others in your niche. Wearing the local attire helps me travel, but it has also helped me stand out among the other travel vloggers out there.

6. Post on YouTube, Facebook, Instagram, Snapchat, X (formerly Twitter), TikTok, and anywhere else that you can. Get your content out to as many places as possible and then connect people to the source content.

7. Titles and thumbnails are half the battle, and you need to get good at them. You want to draw people in at first

glance, showing them what they will learn and why they'll be interested.

8. Do giveaways. Everyone likes free stuff; it helps to build interest and engagement.

9. If something goes viral, that indicates that your audience likes that kind of storytelling. So do more of it.

10. Don't quit. Ever. Keep grinding it out and take time off if need be.

Plus, you can use me (and other creators) as a resource!! Ask questions! And build a community of other vloggers who can help you share your content.

Whether you want to become a vlogger or blogger, don't think that it has to be centered around travel. That is just my avenue and my personal passion in life.

Whatever it is that you enjoy most, you can make content around that. And that is the beauty of the internet and the society that we are living in!

If you love dogs, then you can write or film stories about dogs. If you love lollipops, trees, animals, sports, fashion—or anything else under the sun that you can think of—there will be a market for it online. This opportunity was never around for our parents, our grandparents, or any other generation in history.

JUST START

The hardest part is TO START. Everyone has ideas or thoughts, but actually making that first move is the most important one. You don't need to have all the answers when you are starting—this will fall into place and evolve as you continue finding your voice and your way of storytelling. When I look back on my videos from five years ago, I almost want to cringe because I know that experience made me better. It's all about learning and growing and evolving. There are no shortcuts to success, only hard work and patience. It's the same for any profession, really. You might have heard about the rule of ten thousand hours, coined by Malcolm Gladwell. He states that the key to achieving true expertise in *any* skill is by practicing for at least ten thousand aggregate hours. If you want to become a professional basketball player, or a makeup artist, or an airplane engineer, there's no substitute for the hours spent honing your skills.

THREE RULES FOR MONETIZING CONTENT

Anybody can start a blog or a vlog, as long as you have access to the internet. Not everybody, though, will make money with theirs right away. If you're serious about making money with your content as a side hustle or even your main gig, here are some things to keep in mind.

1. Start with YouTube. If you are interested in monetizing content online, I think YouTube is the best option. Facebook, Snapchat, Instagram, and TikTok also allow you to monetize, but not as much as you can on YouTube. For many people, YouTube has essentially replaced traditional TV, and I believe it will continue growing in popularity because of all the powerful, impactful, and inspiring content available on the platform. (Contrast that with

short-form vertical content like TikTok, which will eventually die out and get replaced by the next social media trend. I'm sure that there is another social media platform in the works right now that is not publicly out yet, but no doubt it will be a game changer for the next wave of content creators.)

Other social media networks, such as Instagram, TikTok, and X (formerly Twitter), are useful to post snippets (or cut downs) of the main YouTube video. And then, you can bring people over to YouTube from these other social media networks, which is a smart idea because YouTube is the main moneymaker. Also, YouTube is also the best platform to engage with your community (it's where many of your diehard fans hang out and watch your content).

I know at first it can feel overwhelming, but the more you begin to share your travels and connect with other people, the less intimidating it feels, and the more you'll feel at home on social media—and in sharing your experiences of the world.

2. The more views, the more money! The rule of thumb is that the more views that come in, the more money you can make through advertisements (on YouTube) and brand sponsors. The ads on You-Tube are those little five- or fifteen-second commercials that play before the video starts, during the midpoint of the video, and after the video—the content creator gets a small amount of money for every time that it shows. On average, every one million views get you about $3,000–$5,000 USD in earnings.

Paying attention to titles and thumbnails is key for packaging your content (in the same way that a book title and cover are the first impressions of the book). And focusing on retention is vital—what will be the "hook" of the story? How can you focus on beefing up the first ten seconds of the video so viewers will choose to stay for the remainder? At the end of the day, you are directly competing with other YouTubers or even traditionally produced TV shows on Netflix.

3. Get brand sponsors. For example, a brand like Sony will pay me to promote their product in my video. The more views that my videos have, the more money that I can charge. When you think about it, this form of advertising makes sense. In the olden days, they had newspapers. Then newspaper ads evolved into TV commercials, billboards in big cities like LA and along interstate highways, and anywhere else to get your name out there. But now, they have trusted experts using and promoting their products, with an audience watching their value in real time.

In the beginning, I sent out thousands of pitch emails to brands related to travel. I would track down specific people in the marketing departments at companies by using LinkedIn and sending them crafty emails. But as time went on, these brands started reaching out to me, and now I have a brand manager who gets on the phone and closes the deals.

WE ARE THE FUTURE

My videos are just another form of mass communication—and with analytics, I can track who is watching, where they are from, what their interests are, etc. Most brands are putting their marketing budgets toward content creators as opposed to mainstream TV ads, because we are the ones who can convert and drive traffic. We have built-in communities around us, which means that people trust us, and they would be more likely to buy a product that we recommend than, say, one they find in Walmart. We have all the leverage!

If I never vlogged the Makushi tribe in the Guyanese Amazon, their story would have never been heard. At least until now, I haven't come across many movies, books, or articles on the lifestyle of this tribe. But after going there for several days, meeting with the people, and hunting for anacondas at night in the rainforest—I learned so much and established a connection with the people in the tribe that I shared with the world.

I love being a messenger on YouTube, and I will continue to do so for as long as I can.

📍 Taj Mahal, India

CHAPTER 13

Be a Part of the World

W hat comes next? Well, that's a good question.

I know some of what comes next for me. As I write this, I finished going to every country in the world about a year and a half ago, and I've put a lot of thought into my future. I know that I want to continue staying in front of the camera and creating content and building my empire. Instead of chasing the "country,'" I will now be chasing the "story," wherever that leads me. I don't have a desire to go back to every country in the world. But I will go anywhere—from Uzbekistan to Australia to Bolivia—to find the story.

> **I just have a desire to keep sharing the good side of humanity and keep educating and inspiring all of you out there to travel. And the more places I go, the bigger my bucket list grows.**

While I was working on this book, I went on the biggest adventure of them all—I got married, as you know by now! Deanna and I took a normal, relaxing beach vacation for our honeymoon. Kidding! Where do you think two travel vloggers would go on their honeymoon? As I shared earlier, we went to Uzbekistan, Dubai, Ethiopia, Rwanda, Uganda, D.R. Congo, and Saudi Arabia. And most of these destinations were by Deanna's request!

I'm excited to keep going in the years ahead. Watch for the videos on YouTube! As of this writing, I have so many places I want to visit: Mongolia is a prime destination, as there are so many special cultures in the Gobi desert and throughout central and western China and Tibet. And though I have been to Siberia, the area is vast, with so many more rarely-seen communities and tribes living in the farthest reaches of our globe. Brazil is huge, and I have never been to the Amazon regions. From northern Chile to southern Chile, there are whole stretches of unknown lands and people—Indigenous tribes who are fighting to protect their way of life in a rapidly changing world. And there is the desert. Do you realize how much desert there is? All across northern Africa, from Namibia to Cameroon, there are tribes living much as they have for millennia, since the beginning of humankind.

To be good humans, it's important to give as much as it is to take. That's why I feel that you should be a good ambassador for your own hometown! In the same way that I suggest making local friends when you travel—to help guide you through cities—you should also reciprocate that in your neck of the woods and encourage visitors. You can host people at your house via Couchsurfing.com or MeetUp.com, be a part of Facebook groups, or simply keep an open mind if you hear that any strangers or friends of friends are stopping by your city/town/village. We have a tendency to think that our hometowns are not that exciting—because we are from there—but to other people, it's a brand-new experience!

In the Pacific, there are a lot of islands that I haven't been to, like French Polynesia, and those islands each have their own cultures and languages. I am really interested in the Arctic communities after visiting a place called Ittoqqortoormiit in Eastern Greenland and Barrow, Alaska (the northernmost town in the USA). Their culture is so fascinating, how they can survive in the bone-chilling cold weather! I also have a mission to visit a province in northeastern Canada called Nunavut, where only thirty thousand people reside. I can't wait to see what life is like up there.

And then there is still so much to learn here in the US. In fact, there are sixty-three, national parks in the United States alone—and I have only been to eighteen of them. I'm also really interested in Native American cultures—no surprise, coming from Arizona. If the Navajo nation was its own state, it would be the twentieth biggest state in the US. That's the beauty of the USA. Driving four hours can bring you to a whole unique culture.

There are many ways to JUST GO in your own community. Here are ten ways in which you can get started!

1. Hit up local events. Look out for things to do in your community that you don't usually attend—festivals, cultural gatherings, food events, and so on. There are tons of ways to explore world communities in every city and most towns in the US.

2. Join local clubs or organizations. It might be a sports club or book club, gardening society, or anything that fits your interests. One of the most important parts of travel is meeting new people—and you can do that anywhere!

3. Volunteer. Check out local charities, non-profits, or community organizations that align with your interests. It's amazing how much you can learn about the world when you become a part of making it a better place.

4. Take a class. I've learned so much on the road, but it was school that inspired me to go there. Taking a class or workshop around something you love can help connect you to

your sense of adventure, even if the adventure is just down the road.

5. Attend a religious or spiritual event. You don't have to believe in a faith to get something from it. Some of my most powerful experiences have happened while celebrating other people's religions. We learn so much about other cultures and the world through others' beliefs.

6. Join a local sports team. Though I have golfed across the world, my local golf course has introduced me to so many people. Connecting with others through sports is its own international language, and you can speak it anywhere.

7. Visit restaurants and coffee shops. You can learn so much about a culture through their food (and coffee and tea!). By visiting restaurants from other cultures, it's like finding a passport to the world—in your own hometown. Plus, who doesn't like food?

8. Social media. It is incredible how much of the world you can see—and how many people you can meet—through social media. Start building your global network today. And you can use my site to do it. I have so many international friends chatting on there all the time.

9. Be a tourist in your town. Sometimes it's amazing how little we know about our own city or culture. Check out local museums and landmarks to find out more about where you live, who has lived there before, and how your own community came to be.

10. Make new friends! You can host your own potluck or party and invite people from your neighborhood, new hobby, sports team, workshop, or community over. By bringing people together, you can create your own global community—in your backyard, literally.

It's amazing how much you can see of the world without leaving your own city. It's always about finding the adventure—and sharing it.

At the age of thirty-one, I don't have any plans to slow down. But whenever that time comes, I will find the next Drew Binsky(s) out there to whom I can pass the torch to become the next travel storyteller.

We could spend every minute of every day of every year of our lives exploring this world, and there still would be more to find. There are always going to be new places to see, even in your own backyard.

> **Once you start to go places, you begin to find the true story of the people and the culture. You begin to understand the true meaning of these places. And it's where the best stories come to be.**

And then you too can begin to share it. You don't have to travel the world to create content. I think that creating content from your own hometown is a great way to showcase unique aspects of your community and make connections (both locally and abroad).

Here are three steps for you to get started with content creation centered around your hometown:

1. Define your niche and purpose. Figure out what you want to focus on—your local culture, history, events, food, or something else? Identifying your niche is crucial to help you focus what you're

filming and how you're going to edit it later. Understanding your purpose will help guide your content creation—and the message you hope to share.

2. Research and explore your hometown. Everything I do begins with preparation—that's what allows me to be spontaneous on the ground. Research your town so you can showcase the hidden gems, untold stories, crazy facts, and amazing people that make your community so interesting. And always stay open—to the stories, the people, and the adventure. You can say yes wherever you are, even when you're at home.

3. Create engaging content. If you want people to watch your content, you need to get their attention. Visually appealing, well written, and engaging stories draw people in. Through storytelling (and great editing), you can make your content relatable and emotionally engaging—and share why this means so much to you. Remember, you might be interviewing or telling the story, but people are ultimately watching because you care about the story you're telling—and you want them to care too.

As you create and share content that showcases the uniqueness of your community and its connections to the world, you'll have the opportunity to build a community of like-minded individuals who share your interests, reaching a wider audience and fostering connections both locally and globally.

The world is a great place. And I'm happy that you were here with me to enjoy it.

When you finish reading this book, I hope you buy a ticket anywhere, whether by bus, train, or plane . . . or hop in your car and head somewhere new. And I hope the moment you start, you discover, and you learn, and you grow, and you meet people. You JUST GO—and then you can't stop.

I've never heard someone say, "I went to Turkmenistan, and I wish I hadn't gone there."

I have never heard of anyone regretting any trip. Traveling only makes you wiser and more connected to other people and cultures.

Because to become more understanding, and wiser, we have to begin to understand ourselves and each other better.

No matter where you go—from Paris to Pyongyang—be courageous. Meet new people and dare to go the extra mile. Let the adventure lead you. Don't be shy. Even if you're introverted, there is nothing to be afraid of. You can go anywhere in the world as long as you remember to be safe, be social, and ALWAYS be spontaneous. Remember that a stranger is just someone you haven't met yet. And as I have found, there are literally billions of strangers across the world who want to share their culture and customs and country with you. They want to share their friendship.

> **When we travel, we have the opportunity to unlock the beauty of cultures across the world, but, also, the wonder of human connection.**

We can either plan our lives away, rushing from A to B thinking that, maybe one day, we're going to achieve C. Or we can JUST GO—and find that the world is always waiting for us. It's been there this whole time. So where is the first place you plan to visit?

I encourage you, as soon as you complete this, to go somewhere, anywhere—and let me know! Please reach out to me on any social media platform @drewbinsky (Instagram, Facebook, Snapchat, X [formerly Twitter], YouTube, TikTok), and I will get back to you. If you go to a place that you previously thought was dangerous or scary, and you realized that it's different—please send me a note! It makes me happy to hear from you and to know that my book inspired you to travel, which is my goal.

JUST GO is a movement of likeminded travelers (or people interested in travel) around the world. It's a place for people to connect, network, and inspire! We've sparked great friendships, marriages, and experiences around the world, and we'd love for you to be a part of it! The best way to join is on our Instagram page (instagram.com/just_go_fam!)

I'll see you out there on the road.

In the meantime, I've got to JUST GO.

BE A PART OF THE WORLD PLEDGE

BY _____, I will travel to _____,
Set Date

_____, and _____.

I will be safe, social, and ALWAYS spontaneous. I will

JUST GO.

Signed,

_____
Signature

_____
Printed name

_____
Date

ACKNOWLEDGMENTS

I owe gratitude to those people in my life who have offered their unwavering support over the years.

First and foremost, heartfelt thanks to my parents, Ellen and Danny. Your encouragement and belief in my abilities have been my guiding light. I'm so grateful to call you both my parents, and I am looking forward to more trips in the future!

To my wife, Deanna, your patience, love, and understanding during the countless hours I spent immersed in traveling are the foundation upon which this book stands. Your support made this journey not only possible but infinitely more meaningful.

To my incredible friends and guides who I met in every country, you not only shared your own cultural wonders with me but also ensured my safety throughout the adventures. Your generosity turned each page of this book into a vibrant chapter.

A special shout-out to my dedicated YouTube and production teams, whose creativity helped transform experiences into visual stories. To Kristen, my cowriter, your keen insights and meticulous work elevated this book to new heights.

And to the remarkable team at BenBella, your hard work and dedication to storytelling have been a cornerstone in bringing these tales to life.

Last but not least, a heartfelt thank-you to YOU, the reader. Your presence and engagement make this journey worthwhile. Thank you for joining me on this adventure.

INDEX

ABOUT THE AUTHOR

Drew Binsky is one of the youngest people in history to visit all 197 countries in the world. He completed this goal at age thirty and is one of about 250 people to do so. He works as a full-time content creator and YouTuber, with an online community of over thirteen million, and his videos have garnered more than five billion overall views. Drew first got the travel bug after studying abroad in Prague during his junior year of college. Then, shortly after graduating from the University of Wisconsin–Madison, he took a job as an English teacher in South Korea, where he lived for two years. During that time, he started a travel blog, which evolved into making travel videos on social media. His main goal is to inspire others to travel and step outside their comfort zones, because the world is a beautiful place and traveling is the best education that you can have! He is from Phoenix, Arizona, where he currently lives with his wife, Deanna, and their pug, Dudoy.